Chris Rettig
14238 Park Drive
Brook Park, Ohio 44142

BEYOND
SYMPATHY

BEYOND SYMPATHY

What to say and do for someone suffering an injury, illness or loss

Janice Harris Lord

Pathfinder Publishing
458 Dorothy Ave.
Ventura, CA 93003
1988

BEYOND SYMPATHY

WHAT TO SAY AND DO FOR SOMEONE

SUFFERING AN INJURY, ILLNESS OR LOSS

By

Janice Harris Lord

Edited By: Eugene D. Wheeler

Published By:

Pathfinder Publishing
458 Dorothy Avenue
Ventura, CA 93003

Copyright ©1988 by Janice Harris Lord
    First Printing 1988
    Second Edition: 1989 Revised

Library of Congress Catalog Card Number: 88-61044

ISBN 0-934793-21-2

DEDICATION

To my mother, Ruby Pettigrew, who died suddenly during the writing of this book, and to my father, Robert Pettigrew. They have joined their children and grandchildren in our own sufferings, never giving trite or simplistic answers, but standing with us as we discovered our own.

ACKNOWLEDGEMENTS

This book would never have been envisioned without the letters, phone calls, and interviews of hundreds of persons in various kinds of pain who were willing to tell me what helped and what hurt as others tried to comfort them. It is they who bring life to these pages, and I wish I could list them all.

Several people have been particularly helpful during the writing and rewriting of the manuscript. Kay Kirman and Sally O'Connor, my colleagues at Mothers Against Drunk Driving, have been an invaluable source of support in talking through the concepts and in fine-tuning the manuscript. Suzan Brooks, Micky Sadoff, Nancy Johnson, Christine Rich, Betty Jane Spencer, Tom and Pat Satterly, Dorothy Mercer, and Ginny Sprang read the manuscript in full for the last edit and provided valuable suggestions.

My husband, Dr. Richard Lord, has devoted many hours to listening, reading drafts, and offering valuable and constructive comment. His support and encouragement, not just with this book, but with all my endeavors is truly a blessing.

Eugene Wheeler, my publisher and editor at Pathfinder Publishing, has been wonderfully patient and supportive. He has handled the manuscript with absolute integrity, careful not to disturb intended meanings. I always feel encouraged after talking with him, a statement few authors can make of their publishers.

Many thanks go to Ingrid Scott for her organizational and editing work on the manuscript; Genie Wheeler for manuscript review, and Joyce Dace-Lombard for her comments. I also thank Susan Bragg of the Family Help Center in Dallas, Texas and Linda Braswell of the Rape Crisis Program in Fort Worth for their assistance with the Family Violence and Rape chapters. I greatly appreciate the cover design by Josh B. Young.

Janice Harris Lord
March, 1989

CONTENTS

Preface

Part I. FROM UNEASINESS TO UNDERSTANDING

> Considering the Level of Care Needed
> Evaluating the Level of your Commitment
> Understanding the Grief of Loss
> Taking Care of Yourself

Part II. UNDERSTANDING THE NEEDS OF PEOPLE IN SPECIFIC SITUATIONS

PREFACE

It hurts to become bereaved, seriously sick or injured, separated or divorced, victimized criminally, to lose someone close to you, be forcibly retired, or have any number of other painful experiences. While the exact kind of hurt depends on many things, most losses involve indescribable emotional pain as well as physical pain. It takes a long time for broken and bruised bodies to heal. It takes even longer for broken spirits to heal.

Sadly, many people who suffer these losses also experience a second injury--at the hands of those who wish to comfort and support them, but don't know how. Out of anxiety or ignorance, they say and do hurtful things. Or worse, they abandon their friend or loved one because they don't know what to say or do.

The goal of this book is to help you to be an effective helper and to prevent second injuries.

The real authors of this book are hundreds of men, women, and children who were willing to talk about what hurt as their friends and family tried to assist them in coping with their emotional and physical wounds and grief. Many of the suggestions came from nearly 300 responses to a questionnaire which was sent to families in which someone had been killed or injured. Other responses came from letters and phone calls. A large number came from support groups of persons who had banned together due to a death or injury in their family, or groups of women and teenagers who had been victims of physical or sexual assault.

While specific pieces of advice in this book are geared toward particular types of painful experiences, certain threads of attitudes and supports weave through them all. Thus, the "Helping Principles" sections are crucial. It is hoped that readers, while tempted to jump to the specific topic of interest to them, will read the book in its entirety. Some duplication has been necessary in order to adequately cover the subject in each situation, but it has been kept to a minimum. A complete reading of the book will provide understanding of the principles underlying the suggestions for helping people in each "Specific Situation."

It is hoped that you will find this book not only "interesting reading," but that it will motivate you to action. In this busy and task-oriented world, it is easy to avoid actively caring for those who hurt. If you take the messages of this book to heart and act on them, you will very likely be rewarded for your experience. Think how it might feel if, when your hurting friend or loved one is later asked, "What helped you the most?", his or her response is "A very special person"...and that person is you.

I welcome you to the adventure of becoming a more skilled helper to someone in pain. It will not be easy, but it may be one of the most significant things you do in your lifetime.

PART I

FROM UNEASINESS TO UNDERSTANDING

CHAPTER ONE

THE FIRST STEP IN HELPING

Someone you love is going through a crisis, and you want to help.

You feel anxious and uncertain. You want to be a source of comfort, but you don't know what to say or do.

You're afraid you might cry.

You don't know whether to go to them, to phone, or to send a note. If you do go, you worry about what to say when the door opens.

You want to know more of the details, but don't know if you should ask.

You wonder if it's wise to mention what happened.

In fact, your frustration may be so great, you are considering doing nothing at all. You rationalize that someone else can do a better job. It might be best to avoid the whole thing, at least for now.

Hold on! People who hurt--whether in sorrow because of a death, facing their own or a loved one's serious injury or illness, coping with a lost love relationship, or even struggling with an unexpected job change or retirement--need the caring attention of family and friends.

> In spite of it all, there seemed to be no limit to the love and compassion my truest friends showed me. They wept for me and with me, held my hand, consoled and watched over my family, and accepted me in spite of my physical and emotional scars. If I live to be one hundred, I will never forget them. And if they ever need my help, I will be there for them.[1]

> Victim of a violent stabbing

Sadly, too many people feel betrayed and misunderstood as they cope with the difficulties of life. They find that their "reliable" friends and relatives abandon them just when they are needed the most.

Caring friends and relatives usually want to help, but fail because they don't know how. As one woman whose child had died said:

> It seemed like people didn't know what to say, so they either said nothing or talked about everything else except what mattered.

You can help. Learning what to say and do is not as complex as it may seem. To be considered a treasured friend who knows how to help is a wonderful thing.

Uneasiness to Understanding

As you think about your friend or relative who is hurting, consider these questions:

1. What level of care is needed?

2. What level of commitment are you willing to make?

3. Are you willing to learn about the grief of loss?

CONSIDERING THE LEVEL OF CARE NEEDED

Begin by thinking about how close you are to your friend or family member who is in pain. If you are close emotionally, he or she may want you to be physically present almost immediately after you hear the bad news and from time to time throughout the duration of their recovery.

Members of a family in which someone has died sometimes say they resent the presence of too many persons with whom they do not feel close. They look upon such people as prying or "nosey."

It seemed so inappropriate that people who didn't know my sister or our family came to the funeral home to stare at her body.

Sister of vehicular
crash victim

4

People I'd never met before came up to me the day of the funeral and talked to me for a long time. They should have had more sense. We needed to be alone with our family and close friends.

Woman whose husband was killed
in an automobile crash

Injured and ill people make similar comments about hospital visitors who do not take the patient's needs into consideration. Patients are more responsive to visitors after they feel better and the initial crisis has softened.

The day of my son's crash, a lot of his friends came to the hospital. They weren't able to help and were actually distracting. What helped the most as his hospitalization continued were cards, brief visits, and people bringing food to the house. It also meant so much when people said they were praying for him.

Mother whose son was seriously
injured by a drunk driver

Since he is an elder in the church, I knew he came to the hospital to visit me because he thought it was the right thing to do. But I felt so bad and was so tired that I could hardly listen to him, let alone respond. He stayed for over an hour talking about things that meant absolutely nothing to me, but I didn't have the energy to ask him to leave.

A heart attack patient who
died three days later

Uneasiness to Understanding

If you are a distant relative or friend, sending a handwritten note may mean more than your presence. Whether you are emotionally close or merely an acquaintance, written notes and brief phone calls are almost universally appreciated. Notes can be read again and again and become a treasured source of support. You can say wonderful things in notes you might not be able to say in person. The best part of a written expression of concern is that the recipient doesn't have to react or respond unless they're up to it and want to.

> The cards and letters meant so much, especially the ones from my sister's friends who told me neat things my sister had done and how much she had meant to them.
>
> > Eighteen year-old whose nineteen-year-old sister was killed

> We received nearly two hundred sympathy cards, and I found myself opening them and looking automatically to the signature without even reading the card. What I did savor, though, and read time after time, were the handwritten notes written conversationally, not just platitudes.
>
> > Husband whose wife had died of a heart attack

Your presence at funerals and memorial services is meaningful to surviving families, even if you only knew the deceased casually. Knowing that their loved one had friends who cared enough to come can be very meaningful to the family. They probably won't remember seeing you or what you said, but when they later look through the registry book, they will be grateful for your attendance. Taking time to attend a funeral or memorial service is a cherished gift.

The fact that so many people, especially his school friends, came to the funeral was very helpful to me.

> Mother whose thirteen-year-old
> son was killed

She would never have believed that so many people would attend her funeral, send flowers, memorial gifts, and cards. It meant so much to us. I only wish she could have known.

> Daughter whose mother died

In contrast to those who experienced deaths, or catastrophic injury or illness, persons experiencing divorce, separation, loss of a job, retirement, and other less traumatic losses, are nearly always eager not only for visits from close friends but from acquaintances as well. Our society has not institutionalized rituals of concern, such as sending cards and flowers, when one gets divorced or loses a job. A few people may offer condolences, but for the most part they will be ignored. They will be very appreciative of notes, phone-calls, personal visits--any expression of care and concern.

One word of caution, however, about divorces, retirements, or other losses which have varying meanings. Don't assume that they are bad news! "How do you feel about it?" is a safer and more respectful reaction than "Oh, I'm so sorry," or "Gee, you must be relieved."

The hurting person's assessment of a loss is more important than the actual loss. For example, a pianist who breaks his finger falls into the category of the "seriously injured." The death of a special grandparent, an in-law, or a friend can be as traumatic as the death of a primary relative.

Among those most overlooked by our society are unmarried, living-together couples, and mates or partners of gay or lesbian individuals who need the same attention generally given to traditional couples and families when trouble comes. Friends can be closer than family in these situations and should be given as much support as the family.

Table I, **Suggested Levels of Contact By Relationship and Type of Loss,** may be useful in determining how emotionally close you are and, thus, how you can be most helpful to your friend or family member who is hurting. If you are very close, you'll <u>want</u> to be physically present. If you believe that your friend or relative wants you there, and you want to be there, by all means, go!

On the other hand, you may dread going for a personal visit, but believe that you should as a sense of obligation or etiquette. If you are not particularly close emotionally, your going may be uncomfortable for both of you. Don't be so hard on yourself. Other expressions of caring may be more appropriate and appreciated.

EXPLANATION OF LEVELS OF CONTACT

Level 1. Be physically present immediately and continue intermittently throughout the grieving period. Assist in talking openly about the loss and give ongoing support.

Level 2. Call from time to time and send personal hand-written notes. Openly acknowledge what has happened. Help with maintenance needs if necessary.

Level 3. Send a handwritten note. Make a contribution to a relevant charity, if appropriate, and ask that your contribution be acknowledged to the family.

TABLE I

SUGGESTED LEVELS OF CONTACT
BY RELATIONSHIP AND TYPE OF LOSS

	Close Family and Friends	Other Friends	Acquaint-ances
Seriously Injured Persons	1	3	3
Loved Ones of Injured	2	3	3
Terminally Ill	1	3	3
Loved Ones of the Ill	2	3	3
Death Following Illness	1	2	3
Sudden Death	1	2	3
Suicide	1	2	3
Rape Victim	1	-	-
Loved Ones of Victim	2	-	-
Child/Elder Abuse Victim	Report to Authorities		
Spousal Abuse Victim	1	-	-
Loss of Love/Divorce	1	2	3
Job Loss/Force Retirement	2	2	3
Loss of Property	2	2	-

EVALUATING THE LEVEL OF YOUR COMMITMENT

Only minimal commitment and effort are required to provide Level Two and Level Three acts of caring. However, too many of us forget to send the notes and make the calls! It may be helpful to mark on a calendar the dates you plan to send something or telephone.

However, let us assume, for the remainder of this section, that a Level One response is needed by your friend or family member. You should now think about your willingness and ability to provide this level of care. The old saying, "you can't be all things to all people" is quite true.

Are other areas of your life fulfilling and energizing enough that you can give both time and emotional support to this person for an extended period of time?

Are you emotionally healthy enough not to be devastated if the person focuses his or her anger about what has happened on you?

Do you think that you can be present and open to the experience of your loved one without becoming overwhelmed yourself (and therefore impotent as a helper)?

Are you free of the need to "fix it."? Are you able to offer what you can but also understand that the major part of recovery is up to the hurting individual?

Can you stand with and help your friend or relative without leading them into building a dependence on you?

If you can answer "yes" to all or most of the above questions and you truly want to help, you can probably be an invaluable source of strength. The next critical question is, are you willing to make a commitment which may have a depth you can't assess and which may take more time than you now think?

If you are, it will help you to know some things about the way people react to hurtful situations in their lives and how they go about grieving their losses, no matter what they are.

UNDERSTANDING THE GRIEF OF LOSS

Most people who are hurting, no matter what the cause, go through a similar grieving pattern. On the other hand, each person's loss and style of coping is unique. The process varies according to the quantity and quality of the trauma experienced. It is surprisingly true that some people handle loss well and recover quickly. These people usually have strong support from family and friends, as well as healthy self esteem. Most of us, though, are deeply troubled by loss and take it hard.

Following are some common reactions to loss. These reactions are not bizarre or abnormal. Many models of "grief cycles" have been developed but most include denial, anger, powerlessness, guilt, depression, and finally acceptance. Persons who experience them should not be afraid that they are "going crazy." However, remaining "stuck" in one reaction over an extended period of time may be reason for concern. Most people who get stuck require professional counseling to help them move on. But if your friend or relative moves from one phase to another, even though there will be times of falling back and moving forth, you can be fairly sure that they are recovering.

Uneasiness to Understanding

Reaction of Denial: "I Just Can't Believe It"

We all know that living involves losses, yet we are never prepared for them. We build, nurture, cherish and protect only to find our dreams shattered by death, destruction, or our lack of ability to heal bodies or relationships. That is human nature. It probably always will be.

Nevertheless, when forced to face a loss, most people can't tolerate the emotional impact of it immediately. Consciously or unconsciously, they don't believe it. The more traumatic the loss, the more likely they are to deny its reality.

Denial is seen most easily in those who have just been told that someone they love has suddenly died or been killed. They often go into shock and report feeling numb and robot-like for hours, days, weeks, or even months. When the body's capacity to feel pain is shut down, so are the other senses. Shock and denial are the body's wonderful way of protecting people from emotional pain that is simply intolerable. Some say they feel almost "out of their body"--observing what is going on rather than experiencing it.

> I kept reciting what had happened, but I wasn't feeling anything. I didn't cry. If I felt anything it was a vague anger at Bob. I was angry at him for dying. How absurd!
>
> Woman whose lover
> died suddenly

When people learn that they have a serious illness, or that a love relationship is ending, they, too, experience denial. They simply don't believe it is true until they are better able to cope. This makes relating to them difficult.

I just can't accept it and keep pushing it into the back of my mind. When something triggers me to think about it, my mind subconsciously says, "No, it didn't really happen." I'm completely scatter-brained and confused. I can't remember things. I continually lock myself out of the car and the house. I just don't think.

Woman whose husband left suddenly

If you are more distant from what has happened, you may accept the reality of it before those closer do. In that situation, you must not try to force the person experiencing pain into accepting it. They will come to grips with it in their own time. However, if your relationship is very close, don't let your frustration with their non-acceptance of reality keep you away. It is important for you to be present and to listen. As people lean into their experiences and talk about them with someone who cares, they more fully come to grips with what is happening. Not talking about it only supports continuing denial.

If you try to convince your friend or family member who seems to be denying reality that their perceptions are incorrect, you will meet opposition. No matter what you say, it may be resisted. Therefore, your task is simple. Just listen. Maintain eye contact and nod to let them know you are hearing what they say. This type of "active listening" will encourage the continuation of the communication and enable more realistic thinking. It does not mean, however, that you agree with everything you hear.

Reaction of Anger: "Oh God! I Never Knew I Had This Much Hatred Inside"

Once the painful reality sets in, many people get angry. As a helper, you may find this very difficult to handle. Angry people are not pleasant to be around. The anger may be focused, or it may be as scattered as a shot-gun blast. If you are trusted, you may find yourself the target of the anger, even though you have done nothing to deserve it. It may be tempting to retreat. Don't!

Perhaps the most difficult part of coping with someone's anger is the number of people who suffer from it. Doctors, nurses, insurance people, lawyers, family, friends, and even the most innocent bystanders can become targets. These people don't deserve it. Even the hurting person knows they don't deserve it, but nonetheless, it rushes forth like the spew of a volcano. It can't be stopped. Angry words, scowling faces, glaring eyes, impossible demands, and fists aimed at walls or people can make even the most understanding comforter want to retreat.

> I'm afraid the people who came to see me in the hospital didn't expect what they found--I had become a snarling, wailing, intensely angry human being.[2]
>
> Stabbing Victim

Being aware that fever and itchy chicken-pox are the source of a child's irritable and exasperating behavior can enable a parent to tolerate it. Also, understanding that the source of your friend or relative's anger is a painful heart will help you be more patient.

Most of us wish that life could be fair. We believe that good people should have only good things happen to them, and bad things should happen only to bad people. The randomness of good and bad life experiences is exasperating. When that randomness attacks us, we feel helpless and out of control--which makes us mad!

It is not fair that incurable illnesses invade healthy bodies. It is not fair that accidental injuries and deaths ravage human beings. It is not fair that lovers, spouses or children decide to leave when so much emotion, time, work, and even money have been invested in those relationships. It is not fair that the elderly have to suffer the indignities of dying.

And certainly it is not fair when these losses come unexpectedly with no time to prepare. Regrets about what might have been said or done if one had the opportunity, can anger and frustrate indefinitely.

Violent victimization at the hands of another may create the ultimate source of anger on the part of crime victims and their loved ones. Families in which a loved one has been murdered or killed by a drunk driver report a rage deep down inside them which takes years to soften. Sometimes it never softens.

> Why did she meet this man--I mean this animal (man is not the proper word for him)? I can tell you seventeen years is not enough for him! I hope he suffers at the hands of other inmates who hate men who murder women. I hope he suffers, just as she suffered when she died of his brutality.
>
> Mother whose daughter's
> boyfriend abused and
> murdered her

Rage and bitterness are also normal responses for rape and assault victims and their families. Catastrophic physical and emotional injury can be as difficult as death for some because so many grieving cycles are involved: first learning about the extent of the illness or injury, later learning new pieces about the extent or permanence of the condition, then attempting tasks and failing. Limbs which get cramped and painful when the weather changes are chronic sources of anger. So are scars.

She snapped at the nurse's aide who took her blood pressure. She barked at her sister. When I brought her some talcum powder she had asked for, she took it out of the bag and threw it on the bed. 'It's too small,' she mumbled.

'You seem angry,' I finally said to her.

'You bet I'm angry! I'm angry because I'm stuck. I don't want to be in this hospital any more. I'm so tired of them telling me how great I look and how well I'm doing. I feel lousy. I feel lousy all the time. All these doctors care about is your blood pressure, your temperature, and the size of your tumor. They don't hear you when you tell them how you feel.'[3]

Daughter of a cancer patient

During this stage, your role is to aid your friend or family member in separating feelings from thoughts and behavior. In life, we feel, we think, and we act. All of our experiences fall into one of those categories. Irresponsible or dangerous behavior, of course, is not to be tolerated. Irrational thinking can be corrected. But feelings are feelings. And feeling anger is a sign of improvement--it means one has passed from numbness and denial back into the human experience.

Regardless of the darkness of the emotions expressed, try not to say, "You shouldn't feel that way". That phrase should be removed from your vocabulary. Feelings are harmless. So are vengeful wishes and fantasies, as long as they don't lead to action.

Most of us get very uncomfortable around expressions of anger because we fear angry persons will do something irrational--verbally abuse someone, break things, hit or kill somebody, or drive too fast and endanger themselves or others. If you think these behaviors are a real possibility, you must intervene. You can do this by acknowledging and accepting the anger, and also helping your friend or family member determine other ways to ventilate the anger-- constructively, if possible.

Some people can "write it out" in journals or diaries, compose poetry, or use other artistic modes of expression. The physically healthy can participate in active sports. Mild exercise such as brisk walking is usually quite helpful. Some join organizations of fellow sufferers for mutual understanding and emotional support, as well as to seek constructive ways of dealing with their anger and helping others.

You can be a therapeutic agent by being available, accepting feelings, and not being frightened by them. Let your friend know that if you were in the same situation, you would be angry too. If the anger does frighten you, say so and ask if the person can assure you that he or she won't harm anyone as a result of that anger.

Reaction of Powerlessness: "I Feel Like I'm a Prisoner of My Fear"

Once your hurting friend has come to grips with the fact that life cannot be counted on to be fair, a troublesome helplessness can evolve. That helplessness is exaggerated if numerous other losses have also been suffered.

Widows or widowers can feel helpless when forced to take on unfamiliar tasks or roles which make them feel awkward and uneasy. A child whose parent has died fears that the remaining parent or even he, himself, may die soon. Powerlessness is experienced by the terminally ill as they face the fact that nothing more can be done to stimulate or assure their recovery. It is experienced by seriously injured victims who realize they have no control over what happened to them and could be victimized again. It is experienced by the survivors of a loved one who has been murdered, as they face the vast unknowns of the criminal justice system.

> The nurses in the hospital and even my family and friends couldn't understand why I was so afraid. I had survived a stabbing. To them it was over. But I felt like my psyche had been mutilated as badly as my body. All they could say was, "Don't be silly. Stop acting like a baby!" And so I tried to bravely be alone and stay calm. I seemed to be asking the impossible of myself.

> Stabbing victim

Your task with a powerless person is two-fold: to accommodate their needs, and to acknowledge that fear and helplessness are natural and can take a long time to resolve. Offer to be with them when they feel vulnerable. Offer to help make their home more secure. Drop in or call at night. Don't ridicule them if they want to keep the radio, television, or lights on. Go places with them when they are uncomfortable going alone. Help crime victims regain a sense of control by obtaining crime reports, applying for financial benefits, and asking questions of investigators and prosecutors until the victim understands the criminal justice process.

Remember that what has happened may make no sense to the hurting person. Vulnerability and fears about the future become very real. Let them know that, considering what they have been through, it is normal to be apprehensive. Say, "It's very normal and natural for you to feel this way." You might even ask them to say it out loud. Also reassure them that they will not always feel this way. They may never forget what happened, but in time the memory won't be accompanied with so much powerlessness.

Reaction of Guilt: "If Only I Had.........."

Saying "If only..." and asking "Why?" are normal responses to loss. The guilt beneath the words, however, is largely irrational. Guilt is also a way of saying, "I should have been in control." It is tied to regrets and self blame. It is a way of trying to gain control over randomness.

> Why me? How could this have happened? Where was God? How could I ever trust anyone again? I wondered why I should even work so hard at recovering, when I would be returning to a world full of monsters like the guy who had tried to kill me. I felt like I might have a nervous breakdown.
>
> Assault victim

As a friend, you may find yourself frustrated and even angered by your friend's insistence upon self-blame for what has happened. It may help you to be more patient with this line of thought if you understand why so many hurting people feel guilty.

To blame oneself at least sets up a clear cause and effect. As bad as it feels, blaming oneself feels better than facing the awful randomness of the evils that befall us. It also goes back to that primitive conviction, irrational as it is but deeply imbedded in our guts, that bad things happen only to bad people. If one can just figure out his "badness," at least it will make sense.

Helping your friend cope with guilt can be frustrating because it is the most difficult component of grieving to give up. Because guilt feelings can run deep, they should be heard and acknowledged. The irrationality of the belief underlying guilt feelings, however, can be confronted gently at a time when the person is ready to talk about it.

Shortly after a loss, it is helpful to simply proclaim, "It's not your fault." Later on, though, when the guilt becomes more deeply imbedded, a more thorough response will be needed. Part of what happened may indeed be their fault, and they will need to separate that out from what is not their fault. You can help sort out the mire of data by asking questions and helping to reconstruct the events leading up to the loss.

For example, sometimes a re-enactment of the event can help. One guilt-ridden paramedic, who had rescued victims from an airplane crash, drove several times from the location where he received the report to the scene of the crash until he was convinced that he had made the original trip in the quickest possible time. He was then able to let go of some of his guilt.

Your task is to ask questions in such a manner that persons feeling guilty can determine their degree of fault, if any, in the situation. "Is there anyway that you could have known?" or "Go over it all again with me" will help clarify the issue. Once their guilt can be assessed realistically, they may be able to set large portions of it aside. People need help to shed the feeling that what happened was all their fault, when, in fact, it wasn't.

Reaction of Depression: "I just wish I could roll over and die."

Unfortunately, sadness and depression are involved in the loss of anything which had meaning and value. The significance of the loss generally correlates with the intensity and duration of the sadness.

Feeling sad or depressed does not mean that one is sick or crazy. It means that he or she may not be hungry, not sleep well, be chronically tired, need to withdraw and not be social for awhile, lose sexual desire, and cry a lot.

Since grief has physical manifestations, some people get sick. They may develop stomach cramps or ulcers. Arms and legs feel heavy. Headaches develop. Blood pressure may increase. Chronic conditions, such as arthritis, may get worse. While these are normal responses, they may require medical attention. Generally, it is not wise to increase dosages of suppressants such as valium unless absolutely necessary. They only hinder the mourning process by delaying it for the future.

Your role is to be available if your friend needs to talk or cry and also to respect the need to be alone. You need to monitor the level of depression, and if it greatly interferes with daily living or lasts so long that you fear health damage, suggest a visit to a physician or counselor. Losing or gaining a significant amount of weight, developing chronic illnesses, spending days at a time in bed, increasing intake of alcohol or other drugs, and growing dependence on prescription drugs are warning signals that your friend may be in trouble.

Reaction of Acceptance: "Now I Have Hope for the Future"

Acceptance does not mean forgetting. To expect one to forget a significant loss is unrealistic. A meaningful loss will always be remembered. But hopefully, the remembering will not always hurt as deeply as it does soon after the loss.

Healthy human beings have an amazing, innate capacity to recover. While "time heals" is a phrase resented by the suffering (because they don't feel as if they will _ever_ heal), there is an element of truth in it. As time passes and as one leans into the pain rather than trying to escape it, light does begin to creep through the darkness. As the famous author, Albert Camus, wrote, "In the midst of winter, I have finally discovered that there is within me an inevitable summer."

Acceptance comes when your friend or family member is able to continue on with hope for the future. Acceptance

21

means feeling better without feeling guilty for it. It means reviving energy, engaging in meaningful work, accepting the reality of what happened, restoring self-esteem, finding beautiful and pleasurable things in life, and being able to enjoy social events. It means being able to laugh again.

Keep in mind that most people who suffer severe losses retain some permanent scars. Just as the more deeply a body is wounded the more noticeable the scar, so it is with our emotional selves. It is very difficult to trust that the world is a safe place after one has been assaulted, raped or catastrophically injured. It is very difficult not to worry about those you love after someone dear has been killed unexpectedly. It is hard to believe that new relationships will work out when too many others have failed or even when one has failed badly.

Grief spasms, sudden impulses to cry or reminisce, will pop up from time to time for years. A certain song, the smell of a certain cologne, someone who is a "look-alike," special holidays, looking through scrap-books and photo albums, and other seemingly innocent events can trigger melancholy and unexpected tears. That is normal and it is healthy. It testifies to the significance of something that once was special. Your support and understanding through these experiences will mean a lot.

Some people who have experienced severe losses say they never again feel quite up to par. Their values change. They experience a sense of chronic sorrow that does not weigh them down particularly, but just keeps them from feeling as "light" as they did before. Helping your friend or loved one understand that these feelings are normal some-times results in their feeling stronger.

The good news is that, except for the deepest of losses, recovery is not only possible but probable. Even better news is that you, as an informed and caring friend or family member, can be a major source of helping in that recovery.

TAKING CARE OF YOURSELF

Care-takers need care too! Therefore, be determined from the beginning not to cast yourself in the role of a rescuer or you can become overwhelmed. Keep the focus on the recovering sufferer--not on yourself as a rescuer.

In order to preserve your self-esteem and stamina, maintain a circle of emotionally healthy friends and spend time with them often. Take time to think of things you enjoy doing that energize you. Then set aside time to do them! It is also helpful to maintain a healthy diet, get plenty of rest, and take stress vitamins.

Know that there will be times when you feel you have failed. Don't expect gratitude for your good works or your efforts. One who is deeply in emotional pain can only focus on him or herself. Believe that your efforts will have made a difference, even though they may not seem to at the moment.

If you are like most people, you will, from time to time, say or do the "wrong thing." When that happens, make amends for it as best you can, and then drop it. What matters is that you have been a true and caring friend and that you did the best you could.

PART II

UNDERSTANDING THE NEEDS OF PEOPLE
IN SPECIFIC SITUATIONS

CHAPTER TWO

SERIOUS INJURY

While serious injury and terminal illness have much in common, they differ in three significant ways: injured victims usually have hope of recovery, or at least partial recovery; the injury was most often someone's fault; and most have a personal memory of the injury.

The issue of recovery is both a source of hope and pain for injured persons. Hope can be dashed if, after a date is set when the victim should be able to perform some function, he or she can't. It is dashed each time a new, discouraging aspect of the injury is discovered. It is dashed when more surgeries are needed. It is dashed if semi-permanent or permanent conditions from a head injury are involved. It is dashed when the victim is finally able to go home, but finds it more difficult to function at home than in the hospital. It is dashed when family and friends abandon the recovering person because they are not comfortable around a "handicapped" individual.

How one handles his or her injury depends on the amount of pain, perceived success or failure on any given day, and the amount of realistic hope one has about the future. Moods vary, making care of a seriously injured person difficult. Anger and frustration can spill over to all the caretakers.

> When she came home from the hospital, we had to face this new situation in a place where we had old habits and memories. We really took the tension and frustration out on each other. Sometimes my attempts to help only frustrated her because she wanted so much to be independent. Finally we both realized that if we were going to adjust, we had to express ourselves verbally before we got to the breaking point. It wasn't easy.
>
> Husband of wife who was seriously
> injured in a vehicular crash

Most injured victims blame themselves for what happened, whether they were actually responsible or not. Focusing on "if only" can be frustrating.

As a caring friend or family member, offering realistic hope without minimizing the experience is critical. Injured victims say that they resent those who say, "You're so lucky to be alive" because they don't feel lucky. To the victim, it feels like a discounting of the pain and suffering they are enduring. They struggle with responses like, "You are feeling better, aren't you?" knowing that the questioner wants the answer to be "yes," when in fact it may be "no." "Time" becomes a four-letter word to the injured when used in these statements: "It will just take 'time'," or "In 'time' you'll learn to live with the pain."

Open ended questions, such as, "Well, how is it with you today?" offers the opportunity for honest disclosure. Instead of the "You're so lucky" response, try "I'm so sorry about what happened to you and your limitations, but I am glad you are alive." While, "Are you okay?" feels like it requires a positive response, "How are you?" opens the door to any response.

Most injured victims who learn to cope and adjust set one goal at a time. You can be of immense support to a victim by sharing celebration of accomplishments which would seem minimal to most people. Knowing that someone else believes "you can do it" is a powerful motivator. But, it is important that you give honest, reasonable recognition of signs of recovery. Don't give excessive praise or label the injured person "an inspiration." The duty to be an inspiration or strong can be an unnecessary burden.

An injury which was someone else's fault adds a complicating twist to recovery. Victims of vehicular crashes caused by someone else, especially if the cause was negligence or drunk driving, usually feel bitter and enraged. Because getting through the day may tax the victim's energy for some time, these feelings may not surface at first. When they do surface, most of the injured cry out for justice. Listen to their deep feelings and let them know that it is normal to feel that way. As is true for survivors of a senseless killing, obtaining some semblance of justice, either through the criminal or civil court systems, often assuages some of the rage.

You can be a valuable asset to your injured friend or relative, with their permission, by contacting the appropriate law enforcement agency for copies of crash or crime reports and contacting the district attorney's office to learn what charges are being filed. If the victim is able to personally contact the prosecutor handling the case, it will not only enhance the prosecutor's commitment to the case, but enable the victim to restore some sense of power over what happened.

After the crash, I really suffered because I felt that my life was no longer under my control. By pursuing the criminal case, I began to feel I again had some control. I found that working hard on my emotional recovery helped me work harder at physical recovery. I felt I was reasserting my control.

Victim of drunk driving crash

Powerful tools in the criminal justice system are pictures of the injury and an impact statement, written or presented orally prior to sentencing, if the offender is convicted. Good physical evidence showing the injuries can help the judge or jury understand their seriousness. It also gives the victim an opportunity to impress the offender with the mayhem he caused a fellow human being. After the assault or injury, victims usually do not come face to face with their offender again until they meet in the courtroom.

You can also help by obtaining information about personal injury attorneys in your community--the ones with the best reputation for winning similar cases in court. Sadly, many injured victims are forced to hire attorneys just to get insurance monies due them.

Dealing with personal memory of the injury offers another opportunity for support. Persons haunted by the accident or event frequently experience nightmares, flashbacks, or night terrors. (Night terrors are violent dreams from which the person awakens, but remains frozen in fear, unable to move or speak while the terror rolls on in their mind.) Being willing to listen to the effect these experiences have on your friend or relative will be valued. If he or she lives alone, you might suggest a one-digit phone dial, so that if a night-terror occurs, he or she may dial the one digit allowing you to talk until the victim fully awakens.

Practical assistance is especially valuable to the injured when they return from the hospital. Many people believe that once an injured person returns home they will be functioning fully in a day or two. Offer specific and concrete help to them. Refer to the section on "Providing Practical Assistance" in this book for suggestions. Continue to offer help until your offer is rejected or is no longer necessary.

If the injured person has children, understand that they will need extra attention. Children are vulnerable and can be shaken by the fact that the person who took care of them can no longer do so. They may be horrified by the physical changes they see in their caretaker. Too much new responsibility too soon for a child may harm his or her development. Giving special attention to the children will not only help them, but be a kind gift to the injured person as well.

Recovery from serious injury depends upon the permanence and extent of injuries, and other factors. More than anything, recovery depends on the courage and commitment the individual has made to following the advice of physicians, no matter how tired and frustrated they feel. Recovery depends also on the injured's capacity to accept limitations which may be permanent. Some people with permanent injury turn inward and cut off social contacts because they are embarrassed or depressed about the injury. Their self image is not that of a noble survivor, but that of a miserable-feeling victim.

As a supportive friend or family member, encourage the injured person to socialize, but don't pressure or insist on it until he or she is ready. Offer to set up links with other similarly injured persons. Support groups are available which can be a great source of hope and encouragement. But don't assume that the person will want to spend all their time with other injured persons. If it is possible, help the injured maintain contact with the social group he or she had before the injury. Doing so encourages a return to a more positive self-image, even though some activities may be curtailed.

CHAPTER THREE

TERMINAL ILLNESS

A terminal illness either draws surviving family or friends closer together or pulls them apart. It places great stress on the best of family relationships.

Most people seek several diagnoses before accepting the fact that their loved one may be dying. Not only is that wise from a physical standpoint, but it provides time for the ill individual and those who love him or her to try to come to grips with it emotionally.

Mood swings are a common denominator in families in which someone is very ill. On some days the ill person will feel positive and up beat. Even though the prognosis may be bad, there may be a special kind of joy at being alive. On other days, when the pain is severe, when sleep won't come, when hopelessness and despair loom, he or she may long for death. Family and friends experience these same mood swings, often coupled with frustration and physical exhaustion if they are primary caretakers.

Terminal Illness

The Dying

While facing a terminal illness is not easy for anyone, it may be most difficult for those persons who have been strong, independent, and autonomous. These people find it especially humiliating to depend on others for care. Their anger about the illness and what it has done can make them very difficult to care for. The anger doesn't stay focused on the illness itself, but spills over on others who may or may not deserve it--family and friends, doctors and nurses, ministers, and others who try to meet their needs.

Besides coping with the illness itself, they worry about other things--about how their loved ones are coping, money, the future, and dreams that will never be fulfilled. Above all, they feel frustrated with losing control.

> We let mother make the decisions about her body as long as we could. Should she take chemo or radiation? Should she have surgery? Should she be placed on life support? Should she be buried with her glasses on or off? These decisions gave her power over the situation and took the burden of guilt off us.
>
> Daughter

People with terminal illnesses grieve not only about the possibility of their forthcoming death, but about many lesser losses. They grieve each time a new, negative aspect of their illness is discovered. They grieve each time they are given hope but that hope fails. They grieve the loss of friends and relatives who stay away because they can't cope. Each grieving cycle may begin with denial, then go through the intertwining dances of anger and sadness, perhaps ending in acceptance.

In determining what to say to terminally ill persons, let them give you the cue on terminology. "Cancer," "AIDS," and "heart disease" are very painful labels to place on oneself. Many victims of these diseases have commented that it takes a long time for them to be able to say the word out loud. There is no need to push the label on them unless death is imminent and reason exists for the person to acknowledge that fact.

In AIDS cases, especially, it is best to be sensitive to the need for confidentiality about the label. Many AIDS victims refuse any suggestion that they reveal the diagnosis because of the social stigma involved. Victims of AIDS will experience enough trauma in dealing with their own shame, anger, depression, and fear and may decide to not open themselves up to the judgments of others. If the diagnosis is revealed, they can suffer a multiplicity of losses. Family and friends who think it's "God's judgment" and totally avoid them, people who fear contact irrationally believing that any touching or breathing can be contagious, threatened or actual loss of housing, job, or membership in some churches and organizations plague these victims.

It is important to assess the degree of closeness you feel to an ill person in determining how best to help. People who are sick or embarrassed about their appearance may want personal visits only from close family, friends and their clergy. Unless you fall into one of those categories, a note, flowers, or a phone call is more appropriate than a personal visit.

Cancer victims who have lost hair and significant weight, or AIDS victims who have suffered weight loss and skin discoloration, are among those who may prefer a phone call when in the mood for visiting.

Often, the person who is dying accepts it before his or her family does. If you are close emotionally, and if you have excepted the possibility of death, you will be wise to bring up the subject. Sometimes, the ill person can be honest and open with a friend but can't with family members because they are upset or are unwilling to talk about it.

"How do you think you are doing?" or "What do you think about your future?" are questions which will open the door. But don't be "pushy." If the person acknowledges that death may be forthcoming, listen to his or her concerns and don't discount them. You can continue to offer hope, as you also accept the possibility of death. Touching is usually welcomed after one has decided to talk about death. To take one's hand and say, "How do you feel about the possibility of death" affords the opportunity for as much disclosure as the person wants to make.

If your friend or family member is comfortable talking with you about death, it is very important that you visit frequently and offer to spend time personally or by phone anytime, day or night. Most people talk about dying only with one or two people. If you are one of those people you need to keep the communication lines open as much as possible. Understand that few people can focus on their own death very long at a time. If they find you open, they will say what they need to say and then move on to something else.

As you talk with the terminally ill about death honestly and openly, be prepared to feel anger toward those who cannot accept it. Many jokes are told and false compliments are given to the terminally ill. Seriously ill people generally don't appreciate being told that they look great when they don't, that they're strong when they aren't, and that they'll soon be "up and at 'em" when they know that they won't. While it may be impossible to screen such comments from those who don't know better, you can honor your ill friend or relative with honest feedback.

Loved Ones of the Dying

In most cases, your care-giving skills will be needed by the close family of the ill person as well. Drop a note to the spouse, parents, or child of the person from time to time, to let them know that you care for them and regret the physical and emotional strain that they are experiencing. Offer to provide practical help, such as sitting with the ill person, sending a cleaning person to their house, caring for children or pets, or running errands for them. Specific offers are more helpful than the well-worn phrase, "Let me know if there's anything I can do."

If you are close to family members, try to schedule some time alone with them to open the door for disclosure about the seriousness of the illness, as you did with the patient. Spouses, parents, and children may desperately need to talk and cry about what is happening. Often, they can't bring themselves to talk about it with the person who is dying or even in his or her presence. It is rather common for family members to cling to hope and denial longer than the patient. If that is the case, let it be. Attempting to push people through the various stages of grieving, even anticipatory grieving, never works. If you are willing to be with them at their particular stage of grieving and allow them to fully experience it, they will be more likely to move forward on their own.

CHAPTER FOUR

DEATH FOLLOWING ILLNESS

You have just been notified of a death. If the death was anticipated, you may be safe in assuming that the family and close friends have given some thought to the impending death. This psychological preparation is commonly called "anticipatory grief."

Both the one dying and those who are now grieving probably didn't believe, at first anyway, that death was forthcoming. They may have been angry, discouraged, and depressed as they thought about it. In the best of circumstances, they accepted the fact before the death actually occurred. It is rare for the dying, and even more rare for family members of the dying, to all reach a degree of acceptance. Each person weaves his or her own way through the stages of anticipatory grieving according to their own inner time clock.

One positive aspect of an anticipated death is that it affords the dying person, as well as loved ones, the opportunity to express their love verbally, be involved together in the final care, and make plans for memorial services. Some of the dying feel humiliated because of the amount of care required. But most survivors say that physically caring for their loved one during the last days meant much to them, even though it was exhausting.

> Being able to care for her physically during her illness meant a great deal to me. I know it helped in coming to grips with her death.

> Husband whose wife died of cancer

Conversely, in some marriages and families, the demands of caring for the dying can be monumentally difficult. Troubled relationships can become more troubled under the stress of illness and death. In these cases, hospitalization, hospice or home care with the assistance of private care or visiting nurses, can help in relieving the burden. Coping with guilt over unhealed emotional wounds can make recovery from grief difficult. Ambivalent relationships and extremely dependent relationships complicate the grieving process.

You can be a valuable support by listening supportively to the frustration and regrets. Your acceptance of the person with the affirmation that he or she need not feel guilty because they are having a tough time can mean a lot.

Sometimes the ambivalence can be so painful that the negative components become pushed into the unconscious and the deceased is placed on a pedesal. If gently nudging your family member or friend back toward a realistic memory is strongly resisted over time, counseling is probably in order.

Under the best of circumstances, when death is anticipated, all things needing to be expressed are said, and loved ones are able to be physically present until the end. However, even then, survivors are often surprised at the intensity of their grieving. They may experience denial again when a death actually happens, even though they thought they were prepared. They may feel anger that death was so painful or that the death came differently than anticipated. Most find that even if anticipatory grief was handled well, a new grieving cycle begins when death finally comes. It seems to be a part of human nature that emotionally healthy human beings resist death, even when it comes in the best of circumstances. That is probably as it should be.

Survivors may have trouble coping with the lingering memory of the pain and distress that the deceased experienced before death. The agony of cancer which ravishes bodies, coupled with the painful treatment to counteract it, seem unfair. Slow deaths with prolonged deterioration of mind and body are excruciating not only for the one dying, but for the family. Those intimately involved, including the person dying, may wish for death long before it comes. Often the dying person is ready for death before the family is ready to let go.

Reminiscing about happier, healthy days and memories of the person as a fully functioning individual will help diminish the images of death. They also affirm the contributions the deceased made and neutralize the helplessness of the last days.

The death of a child may be especially difficult to endure. This holds true even if the child is an adult child. Parents who lose children often quote from the New Testament, "And thy own soul, a sword shall pierce." These are the words of the prophet Simeon to Mary, the mother of Jesus, in anticipation of the death of her Son.

It feels terribly "wrong" to be pre-deceased by one's child.

It's so wrong, so profoundly wrong, for a child to die before its parents. It's hard to bury our parents, but that we expect. Our parents belong to our past; our children belong to our future. We do not visualize our future without them. How can I bury my son, my future, my next in line? He was meant to bury me![1]

Father whose son died in a
mountain-climbing accident

Because of feelings that their child was cheated, it is important that the child's life be remembered in special ways. Mention his or her name often. Consider establishing a permanent memorial, such as a scholarship, or write a memorial poem about the child. Mention that support groups, such as Compassionate Friends, exist in most metropolitan communities to help parents cope with the death of a child.

Some deaths carry emotional stigma, which add another layer of grief to survivors. Judgments about smoking, drinking, vocational choices, and lifestyles can color the support given to the dying and their family if the death was believed to be the result of irresponsible behavior.

AIDS may be the most extreme example in our day. Judgment that all victims of AIDS have been involved in deviant sexual activity or drug abuse is rampant. The presumption is that AIDS victims brought it on themselves and, therefore, they and their families require differential treatment. How, where, or why a human being contracted AIDS is irrelevant. Their grieving families needs the same support as others.

Most survivors are surprised at their need to sanctify the deceased when death comes. It appears almost mystical that in the twinkling of an eye, most negative feelings are forgotten and positive memories of the loved one's attributes surface. This is not abnormal.

Death Following Illness

It is important to remember that the bereaved need your attention, even though anticipatory grieving was handled well and some degree of relief was experienced when death finally occurred. If you are emotionally close, go to the home, remembering that your very presence will mean more than what you say. Join the family's sorrow with a statement like, "No matter how well you were prepared, facing death can't be easy. I'm sorry." Attend the funeral, take in food, and send flowers.

Since survivors love to be reminded of the "good times" of their loved one, share these memories in a note sent after the funeral. Far more cherished than pre-printed sympathy cards are handwritten notes which begin, "I'll never forget the time _____" or, "Let me tell you why _____ _____meant so much to me." A handwritten note of special remembrances will be deeply appreciated, even from those who were not close enough to make a personal visit to the home.

Mark on next year's calendar the birth date and the death date so you can remember in a special way. Very few people remember the anniversary date of a death. For those dearest to the deceased, however, that date is indelibly imprinted on their minds. They will dread it. Many experience a resurgence of sadness and depression not only on the death anniversary date, but for weeks preceding it. To be remembered on these dates with a note, flowers, or other appropriate gift, lets them know that they are not alone in remembering.

On October 4, our son's first birthday after he had been killed, we went to church for a mass said in his memory. Afterward, a nun from our church asked if I'd like to go to breakfast. We no sooner sat down in a booth when she asked, "What were you doing twenty-two years ago today?" That was one of the most memorable days of my life. I was allowed to cry, laugh, and share some very special memories. This became a ritual every year. How lucky I am to have such a special friend!

> Mother whose son was killed in
> a vehicular crash

If the death resulted from a stigmatizing illness, follow the lead of family members. For example, if you have heard that the victim had AIDS but the family has not acknowledged it, refrain from mentioning it. Support them just as you would any grieving family who lost a loved one to a terminal illness. If they have acknowledged it, and you are emotionally close, plan to spend quality time with the survivors who will talk with you about it. Sadly, they will find few people who are comfortable in addressing the issue or who will help them express their feelings about it. Some of their friends may abandon them out of irrational beliefs that they, too, may have AIDS. Listen to the anguish, anger, and frustration. Just knowing that you care and that you are willing to understand the complexity of their pain will be comforting to them.

CHAPTER FIVE

SUDDEN DEATH

Those whose loved one died suddenly, frequently lament that the most difficult part for them was not being able to say "Good-bye," "I'm sorry," or "I love you."

Deprived of the opportunity for "anticipatory grieving," discussed in Chapter Four, the shock of a sudden death can leave survivors spinning in a spiral of disbelief for days, weeks, or even months. Most people exhibit physiological shock symptoms when confronted with the news. Many regress to one of the two basic fear responses--fight or flight. Some literally begin to physically assault the law enforcement officer, doctor, or other news-bearer. Others scream, run, or faint.

Unanticipated still-births and SIDS (Sudden Infant Death Syndrome) fall into this category and are among those most frequently overlooked. Many parents whose babies died say that family and friends expect them to easily forget because they "didn't have time to get to know the child." This is not true. Nine months of pregnancy, the extra body-weight and accompanying fetal movement, the planning for the baby, the hopes, and the birth experience, all add up to a tremendous loss when, suddenly, the baby no longer exists.

> I was amazed at how many people treated our baby's death as if she had never been born. Their silence was terribly hurtful. Even a sympathy card would have helped so much.
>
> Mother whose daughter died
> two days after birth

Most mothers, and some fathers, speak of the emptiness they feel physically after their baby has died. Some experience it as a hollowness inside their bodies. Others indicate that their arms literally ache to hold a child again.

Remember that the child was indeed a person. Ask the parents to tell you about the child. If the child lived long enough to be named, refer to him or her by name. Send a sympathy note or flowers. Above all, don't pretend that it didn't happen.

> When people ask me how many children I have, I always have to decide whether to say "two" or "three." It depends on whether I'm strong enough to cope with their response when I say "one died." I have to sneak off to the cemetary because even my family thinks I should forget her by now.
>
> Mother whose newborn died
> several years ago

Other sudden deaths are the result of heart attacks or strokes. While the condition may have allowed some preparation, most people cannot fully grasp the threat of death. The "if only's" are likely to plague the closest survivors for some time. They will wonder what they did or didn't do which resulted in the death.

Encourage the closest survivors to obtain copies of medical records and the autopsy report, if one was performed, and schedule an appointment with the attending physician to explain what caused the death. Usually, nothing could have been done to prevent it. However, if the survivor was in any way responsible, it will be helpful to know, so that he or she need only accept the appropriate amount of guilt. Separating legitimate guilt from illegitimate guilt can be a very healing experience.

> It wasn't until I got the death certificate, looked up all the words in a medical dictionary, and talked with the doctor who was with her when she died, that I was finally convinced that there was nothing I could have done.
>
> Husband whose wife died of
> a heart attack

Many families who have experienced a sudden death, later realize that the avoidance of a lengthy, painful, terminal illness is a positive aspect of what happened. Let them come to this conclusion on their own, however. To be told, "It's such a blessing he didn't suffer" doesn't seem like a blessing when one is longing for the loved one to return to life. Instead, join with the family in their suffering. Share their pain and sorrow without attempting to talk them out of it. "Your heart must be breaking," accompanied by an embrace, will be better received than, "You shouldn't be taking this so hard."

Sadly, too many sudden deaths are the result of violence. Vehicular crashes, murders, and other homicides require loved ones to not only cope with the suddenness of the death, but to come to grips with the mutilation of their loved one's body. That factor is probably more painful for survivors than victims. Many people who have recovered from trauma say they did not experience physical pain for some time.

Human beings have personalities. Most people believe that they have spirits or souls. But bodies are important, too. No matter how assured one feels that their loved one's spirit or soul resides in Heaven, they are anguished because the body was violated. They may sorrow deeply over each wound that is apparent if the casket is opened. Even more devastating is the mental image of the person if it is not possible to view the body. Imaginations can be more gruesome than the real thing.

Understand the significance of what has happened to the body. Do all you can to see that the deceased person's body is honored. Pass along old or recent snapshots of the person which the family may not have seen. Ask if you could go along on cemetery visits and take flowers. If a permanent memorial of any kind is developed, suggest that a recent photo of the person be included.

At some point, the family may decide to view morgue photos or file photos which newspapers or television stations may have taken following a crash or murder. Custodians of these photos are often reluctant to release them because of a desire to protect the family from undue emotional pain. However, most survivors know what they can handle. If they decide to see them in order to clarify unanswered questions, to confirm the reality of the death, or other reasons, they should be allowed to do so. In these cases, families should be told what to expect so that they can make an informed choice. A good friend is sometimes needed as an advocate to obtain pictures and to help prepare the family by looking at them first.

I finally decided I wanted to look at the pictures of my Mother who had been murdered. So I asked my best friend to go with me to the Police Department. When I asked to see the pictures, I was refused. However, the officer said that my friend could go into another room and look at them. When she came out she was in tears. Those

45

tears gave me the answer I needed. Her willingness to do that is the most compassionate thing anyone has ever done for me.

Daughter whose Mother was brutally murdered

Coming to grips with the senselessness of a sudden, violent death may be the most difficult task of mourners. Accidents happen. However, if a loved one was killed by a drunk driver or a demented individual who should have been in an institution, bitterness and rage can become unbearable. Clearly someone was at fault. Having the intensity of those emotions normalized can be a blessing. Many people fear that they are "going crazy" when feeling intense hatred and vengeance. One of the most helpful things that you can say is, "If I were in your shoes, I think I would feel the same way." Helping your friend or family member join a support group of people who have experienced a similar loss can be very helpful. Mothers Against Drunk Driving and Parents of Murdered Children are among these groups.

People whose loved one was killed as a result of criminal misconduct may have to struggle through the criminal justice system maze. Most find this a frustrating and humiliating experience. Again, support groups such as those mentioned above are invaluable in helping families understand what to expect from the criminal justice system and how to interact with it. Many district attorney offices and police departments now have Victim Assistance Programs which can provide information about the criminal case.

It is important to understand that the sudden killing of a loved one is an extremely draining and compelling experience. Many feel almost driven to "do something," although they don't know what. They cry for justice as a way to make sense of a senseless act. Helping them obtain copies of police reports, investigations, and autopsies can facilitate understanding. Obtaining materials about the criminal justice system and criminal code books from a university library can be helpful, too.

The more bizarre and senseless a death, the more both the bereaved and their supporters may try to make something positive out of it. As a helper, be cautious about doing this, because the trite phrases meant to help, such as, "It must have been God's will," "You're young--you'll find someone else," and "You're lucky to still have other children," are deeply resented by the suffering.

As a caring friend, stand by them as they endure the pain rather than try to talk them out of it. Other acquaintances and relatives will withdraw their support too soon. Many people whose loved one was suddenly, violently, and senselessly killed, grieve intensely for several years. Most say they never fully recover. Make a commitment to stay in touch, not to be discouraged or frightened by intense feelings, and to keep talking with them about the departed loved one.

CHAPTER SIX

SUICIDE

Although the aftermath of a suicide is similar to that of other sudden, violent deaths, it differs in several significant ways. Perhaps the most painful aspect of a suicide is acknowledging that it was the victim's choice. To a survivor, that realization leads to the question, "What did I do or not do that caused his or her life to be so unbearable that suicide was seen as the only way out?"

The answers can be so painful that family and friends may need to float in a smoke of denial for some time, trying to believe that it was an accident. If that is their need, it should be honored. Initially, it is best to approach the family as you would any grieving family with no questions asked. Extend your sympathy with open arms, and send flowers, attend the funeral, send a special note of remembrance of the deceased. Don't label the death a suicide until the family does.

If you are like most people, you want to know why and how the suicide was committed. These questions are best left unasked as you attempt to comfort the bereaved. While they may or may not know exactly how the suicide was committed, it is unrealistic to expect them to know the details about it. Bits and pieces of evidence and speculation may be put together during the weeks and months following, but it is impossible to ever know the many intertwining variables that lead one to commit suicide.

Above all, don't blame the family for the deceased person's choice to end his life. Don't imply by question or comment that close family or friends may have been responsible. They will suffer enough guilt on their own. Close family members will feel guilty for missing suicidal signals or not taking observed clues seriously. They will feel guilty for not being available if a final call for help was made. They will feel guilty if they allowed the suicidal instrument to be available.

If, as time passes, you believe that the family has denied reality, or feels too much responsibility, you can gently nudge them toward reality. The actual cause may have been physical or mental problems, an unwanted major life change, a highly self-critical personality, low self esteem, the fantasy that death really isn't death, or combinations of the above. You can help family and friends understand that suicide is an extremely complex decision and that the person responsible for the suicide was the victim, not the family.

Those intimately involved with a suicide victim are prone to numerous "second injuries." Insurance representatives, law enforcement officers, coroners, lawyers, and sometimes the media, probe for information in such a way that survivors believe their integrity and moral character are being challenged. Regardless of the actions of outsiders, it is usually best for the family to cooperate with them, and to understand that their professional role is fact-finding, not emotional support. Not only will this frame of reference help family and friends feel some power in a powerless situation, but they can obtain valuable information if they cooperate.

Sometimes, unconsidered rationales which help explain the suicide may be uncovered. Autopsies can reveal bodies racked with pain, disease, high blood concentrations of alcohol or other drugs. Investigations can reveal unknown pressures at work or other environmental circumstances. The more factual data obtained, the less blame one needs to put on oneself.

If the suicide is newsworthy, you might offer to be the spokesperson to the media, thus protecting those most intimately involved. A simple, written statement such as, "The family is experiencing deep grief because of the death of their loved one and chooses to refrain from public comment at this time," handed to the media can provide valuable protection for the family.

Continue to remember those closest to the victim from time to time with a note or other expression of concern throughout the year. As in the case of any traumatic death, anniversary time will be especially difficult.

The family may be ostracized or abandoned by their friends because people don't understand the complexity of suicide or how to respond to it. These reactions, coupled with the guilt and anger they feel, can be devastating. Their self-esteem can tumble. Spend time with them, allowing free talk about the victim. Refer to him or her by name. Listen to the anguish, guilt, and anger, and accept what you hear. Gently nudge them with questions to help them understand that the suicide was not their fault. If they were responsible in any way, help them understand that their part was only one portion of the many components that led to the suicide. The final choice was the victim's. A helpful comment might be, "The suicide was a decision he made. No doubt, he felt it was the right decision."

Persons in families in which someone has committed suicide are unfortunately, more prone than others to suicide themselves. Refer to the "Preventing Suicide" Chapter if you sense that suicide is an option.

CHAPTER SEVEN

RAPE

Rape is embarrassing and humiliating, not to mention terribly frightening. Rape victims are plagued with fear and self-doubt. They wonder how they allowed themselves to be vulnerable to such a violent act. The fear they experienced during the rape, regardless of whether or not weapons were involved, may be more significant in their recovery than the degree of physical injury they suffered. Most feared that they would be killed during or after the rape as threat and intimidation are the key weapons of a rapist. Many rape victims experience a kind of "frozen fright" during the threats and assault, literally rendering them helpless. Unconscious "frozen fear" or conscious cooperation can be a survival strategy. Fighting back sometimes leads to escalating violence.

I left my home to walk the three blocks to work. It was very cold outside. I heard his footsteps behind me and when he got to me he asked, 'Where are you going?'

Rape

> 'To work,' I responded.
>
> 'You're going no place,' he said as he aimed a gun at my forehead. He dragged me backwards by the neck, to a drainage ditch and raped me. He then urinated on me and dragged me to the top of the hill where he cut all my clothing with his knife and raped me again. Before he left, he slit my trachea. I tried to stay calm and didn't resist. I'm sure that's what saved my life.

> Registered Nurse who was raped

Rape victims fear not only being raped again, but they fear the responses of those who care about them. Take care to avoid the "why" questions, because they imply that the rape was the victim's fault. "Why were you out alone at that time of night?" "Why didn't you fight him?" "Why didn't you scream?" or "What were you wearing?" will only push the victim deeper into his or her shell of self-doubt.

If you're only an acquaintance, you will be wise not to mention the rape. Most rape victims talk about what happened with only a few people. Some want to tell the story to anyone who will listen. Some don't want to talk about it at all.

If the victim chooses to talk with you about it, the most important thing to remember is that he or she desperately needs to hear that you believe that the victim did the right thing and that the rape was not his or her fault. The simple fact that the victim is still alive is proof enough that the right decisions were made. You may be surprised to learn that the victim has a somewhat elated feeling which surfaces intermittently along with the fear and humiliation. It usually means that, in spite of what happened, she is extremely grateful to still be alive.

The victim of rape needs calm, steady reassurance. Begin by indicating how sorry you are it happened. It will help the victim more to talk about the fear for his or her life than to talk about the explicit sexual activity.

The victim may deny, at first, the reality of what happened. The words "rape", "sexual assault", and "sodomy" carry a great deal of stigma for both sexes, but especially for men and the elderly. Don't use these words until the victim does. It is not as important to focus on what happened physically as on what was felt emotionally.

Loss of control may be the most frustrating component of rape. Some feel that rape is a form of murder because it can destroy the will and the spirit. It is important, therefore, to help the victim regain control of his or her life. Your ideas should be couched as suggestions and questions, rather than telling what to do. The following are suggested:

o   "I'd like to hear about it when you feel you're ready to talk about it." When that time comes, be willing to hear the story over and over again, as telling it helps gain mastery over it. It also helps bring to the surface memories that may have been previously repressed. These memories can help assure the victim that the rape was not his or her fault and may also help with the criminal investigation.

o   "Do you think you'd be more comfortable if someone stayed with you tonight?"

o   "What do you think about calling the Rape Crisis Center?"

o   "What ideas do you have for feeling less afraid?"

o   "Have you been back in touch with the criminal investigator to see if the offender has been picked up (or charged)?"

o   "Have you considered the pro's and con's of filing a civil suit against the offender?"

As enraged as you may be, and as clear as your mind is about wanting criminal and civil cases filed, those decisions must be left up to the victim. Your own needs for justice can actually thwart the victim's recovery if he or she can focus only on his or her own pain. While many victims believe that strong prosecution of the offender helps their recovery, others decide that the embarrassment and humiliation experienced during depositions and a trial are not worth it. Again, these concerns are usually exaggerated for male and elderly victims.

After the initial crisis, most victims will appreciate your ongoing concern as long as you do not try to minimize the experience with comments like, "It's time you forgot about it", "You've got to get on with your life," or "Aren't you over that yet?" Genuine expressions of concern, such as "How are you handling your victimization now?" or, "How do you think you are coping with your assault?" allow the victim to understand that you remember and care but leave the choice about disclosure up to him or her.

If you are a close friend or relative, remember to express your concern for the rape victim's spouse, parent, or significant others. These "secondary victims," as they are sometimes called, often suffer greatly as a result of the rape. They will need to talk about how it affected them. In many cases, counseling will help them cope with the violence of an act upon someone they love and whom they were unable to protect.

CHAPTER EIGHT

FAMILY VIOLENCE

Most people who become aware of violence within a family are extremely concerned and yet apprehensive about what to do. They fear calling authorities because they are afraid that the family will find out who called. They fear intervening because it seems intrusive. And yet, they can't bear to stand idly by as the abuse continues.

Violence within families is, sadly, a large problem in America.

o   Approximately 1 million children were abused and neglected to the extent that protective service cases were opened in 1986. At least 1,200 child fatalities were reported.[2]

o   Every year 3 to 4 million women are battered in their own homes. More than 4,000 are killed by their husbands or lovers.[3]

Family Violence

o Between 600,000 and 1 million elderly persons are abused every year. In 75% of the cases, the abuser lives with the victim.[4]

Child and Elder Abuse

If you suspect abuse or neglect of a child or elderly person, the correct course to take is to report your concern to the Protective Services Division of your state or local Public Service Agency (Welfare Department). Your call usually will be granted anonymity. Trying to intervene yourself can cause more trouble for the victim. If you consider the situation an emergency, call the police. The numbers for the above agencies are located in your directory, or you can call 911 if that number is used in your community for emergencies.

Battered Women

You are not required by law to report suspected spousal abuse although your heart may be breaking when you realize that someone you love is being abused in his or her own home. The term "battered" means more than physical abuse. It includes psychological isolation and intimidation as well as violence. In some cases the emotional abuse is enough to warrant the label "battered" even though physical violence may be minimal or absent. Some men are battered although the larger percentage of victims are women.

Many physically and emotionally abused victims are unable to label themselves as "battered" in spite of countless and chronic abuse. Thus they don't see themselves as crime victims.

Most battered women, regardless of their income, intelligence, or socio-economic status, become convinced that they deserve the treatment they receive. Batterers are usually insecure and demand the impossible of their wives or lovers. They want their house immaculately clean, meals exactly on time, children well-behaved, and women attentive and compliant. They do not want their wives or lovers to have friends because they fear it will detract attention from them. They sometimes refuse to have a telephone in the house. If the women fail to live up to these expectations, they are abused and made to feel that they deserve it. Victims try repeatedly to "get it right" so that they won't "deserve" to be punished.

Battered victims frequently try to hide their injuries because they are a source of embarrassment. Deep inside, they feel ashamed that they allowed themselves to be abused, so they hide it. In order to keep their ego intact, they tell themselves that it is not really "abuse" or "battering" and that their husband or boyfriend did not mean to hurt them. The batterer's response usually supports this belief. Many are extremely remorseful following an assault and promise never to do it again. These promises enable battered women to stay in their relationships as long as they do, and to return often after leaving. One study revealed that most battered women are attacked 35 times before they file charges.[5]

The confusion, minimizing the injury, and the willingness to forgive so frequently make intervention difficult. Staying with such a victim until a solution is found takes much time and patience.

It was a year from the time she brought her boyfriend home and when he killed her. Whenever they came to our home, he was quiet and sullen and frequently made us all uncomfortable. During the summer she called home twice, once to tell me that her ear was black and blue, and once to tell me he had tormented her by bringing an old girlfriend into their home. She was hysterical both times, but she later told me he had apologized and she forgave him. Christmas Eve he got drunk and beat her until she was black and blue all over. But again, he returned with a cry for help and promised never to do it again. So, once again, she took him back. I was scared for her, but never imagined that he would kill her two months later. I worried about her and called her every few days, but he didn't like that and said I was interfering. How I wish I had interfered more.

Mother whose daughter was
murdered by her boyfriend

As a caring friend or family member, if you suspect abuse begin by calling a Domestic Violence Program or Women's Shelter in your community to learn of programs and resources available. It the victim decides to leave, you may want to open your home to her as a temporary haven. If you cannot, she will need a plan for leaving as most shelters have waiting lists. For financial or other reasons, she may feel that leaving is impossible. In that case she needs information about counseling programs both for herself and the batterer.

Document your concerns and your information and plan to gently confront her with the evidence as you see it when you can be alone with her. Don't be afraid to ask her directly about injuries you have observed. Let her know that you believe she is being abused and why. If she is able to admit it, offer to help her explore options for staying but getting hurt less often, or for leaving.

Above all, don't support her claims of "deserving it." The fact that she was unable to comply with the batterer's expectations does not mean that she deserved to be abused. Help her see that even if she loves him, she does not need to be battered. If there are children in the home, help her explore the impact of her abuse on them.

If she decides to leave, help her make plans to actually leave and to find a place to stay. It is usually best not to tell him she is leaving, She should leave quickly at a time when he is away. Suggest she call a Domestic Violence Program or Shelter to learn the procedure for obtaining a protective or restraining order unless or until she considers filing for divorce.

Do not risk discussing the abuse on the telephone with her and do not ask Domestic Violence Centers or Programs to mail literature to her home, as this information can escalate the abuse.

Seek her out often and build up her self-esteem. This is as important after she leaves, as it is while she is deciding what action to take. Build on the relationship you have with her by listening carefully and patiently. Let her know that you accept her and understand that she may now feel so intimidated that it is hard for her to think clearly and plan rationally. Help her realize that she deserves more out of life.

At the same time, avoid the rescuer role and realize that her life is her own. You may love her, support her, confront her with compelling evidence, and help her look at options, but the decision to stay or leave is hers.

CHAPTER NINE

LOSS OF A LOVE/DIVORCE

People who are divorcing, and those suffering the loss of a love, are among the loneliest of all. They frequently lament that no one reaches out to them. They assume that if no one mentions the divorce or separation, no one cares. In actuality, their friends and acquaintances may care very much but probably can't decide what to say, so they say nothing. It is tricky to try to say the "right thing" to one who is going through a divorce or separation.

Many people believe that it is immature to "take sides," and that both partners should be equally supported. That may be true in some situations, but everyone going through a divorce needs at least one or two friends who will be fully supportive of them, listening attentively at all hours to the outbursts of anger, frustration, pain, and loneliness. They need someone they trust to "wallow with them in the pits." If you are a very close friend, it is noble to be fully supportive of one or the other.

I valued so much my one good friend who let me bitch and gripe without trying to "fix it." Seems like most people think they should act like a therapist in these situations, but that's not what I needed. I needed someone to hear me out and just be with me.

Man going through a divorce

As a more distant friend or acquaintance, you may genuinely care for both, want to be supportive of both, and may puzzle over what to say.

Some responses should be avoided. One is "Oh, I'm so happy for you. I never could understand how you put up with him." This puts the divorcing individual in an awkward position. While the comment may affirm the present situation, it evaluates the person as exceedingly stupid or weak for having made the choice to live with the person as long as they did. Also, no matter how final the story may sound, the possibility of reconciliation always exists, and if it is achieved, you can be certain that your comment will be shared, thus ending any possibility of your continuing friendship. Finally, the statement greatly discounts any pain the divorcing individual may be experiencing. The person may agree with you that he or she is "better off" or "deserves better," but another part of him or her may be hurting, lonely, and afraid. It is probably the second part which he or she most needs to express, and it will not be expressed following such a comment.

Conversely, "Oh, I'm so sorry," cuts off any expression of relief that the divorcing may wish to express. It also may cut too soon into the divorcing person's denial. Many people have filed for divorce or been filed upon who feel that an actual divorce is a remote possibility. Statements like, "You must be having an awfully difficult time," will also leave the divorcing person who is doing well at a loss for words.

Loss of Love

So what do you say? More than anything, divorcing persons need validation of their feelings. You cannot validate them if you don't know what they are. Therefore, a caring question, followed by attentive listening, is the response of choice. "How are you finding living alone?" will open the door to free expression, positive or negative. The honest answer will probably include both. Knowing that you have no preconceived ideas about how the person is doing will invite not only honesty in response, but will serve as a gentle encouragement to think about it and talk about it.

As is true in encouraging expression of feelings regarding all kinds of losses, asking open-ended questions (those that can't be answered with "yes" or "no") and a willingness to share one's own feelings is a very workable and validating process. In a recent study in which persons receiving counseling were asked what qualities and techniques of their therapists helped them the most, their responses were (1) "willingness to listen to how I felt," and (2) "willingness to share their own personal feelings and thoughts."[6] Anyone can do that. The mastery of the skill comes in the combination of the two. Too many open-ended questions causes one to seem "nosey" or like an interrogator. Too much self-revelation on the part of the friend is boring and draws the focus away from the one who needs to be talking.

People in the process of separating may be uncomfortable talking about their feelings in detail in public places. If you find them responsive to a few open-ended, caring questions, especially if you have some personal experiences you would like to share, ask to schedule a lunch or other quiet setting together where you can share more fully.

You must understand, too, that not all divorcing people want to talk about it. For some it is too painful. For some it is too complex. For some it is an embarrassment which they wish to handle alone. If so, you must respect that and leave them alone. Let them know that you are thinking of them by asking how they are doing when you see them in a group, invite them to your home for a meal, and drop them a note from time to time. But failure to respond openly to a couple of open-ended questions is your clue to leave the subject.

Try to accommodate the practical needs of the person now living alone. Giving a casserole to one who is unaccustomed to cooking can be a blessing, especially if it can be frozen. An offer of free baby-sitting can mean a great deal. An invitation to a gathering in which there are a number of other single people can help begin the establishment of new friendships. Although touchy, the offer of money can be a wonderful support if you are able. Fund offers should be couched in phrases such as, "In case you are having some cash flow problems right now, it would make me feel good to help you out." An offer can be made then without embarrassment on either person's part.

CHAPTER TEN

JOB LOSS / FORCED RETIREMENT

We love and need those things which make us feel important. Jobs can make people feel important. When those jobs are gone, it is normal and reasonable to grieve.

Most people say that their families are the most important things in the world to them. However, when one looks at their priorities and behavior, it becomes apparent that they are just as committed, or more committed, to their work. Most work places offer emotional rewards for jobs well done. The praise and support of colleagues spells respect, and sometimes that kind of respect is lacking in the home. Some people feel that they contribute positively to the world through their jobs; they can see that what they do or produce makes a difference. In any case, work is where most people spend the greatest part of their lives.

As a supportive friend to someone who was forced to retire or leave a job, create the opportunity for expression of sadness and anger. People assume that retirement is a pleasurable event. For many, it is. Receiving the gold watch and making jokes about how the retiree will now spend his time are traditional components of retirement parties. But little thought is given to those who are not happy about it. Rarely will someone say:

> "How do you feel about no longer working?"

> "How is it for you to wake up in the morning with no schedule to follow?"

> "I guess there are good things and bad things about not working."

Statements such as these are helpful because they offer an opportunity for expression without assuming that what happened was all good or all bad. As suggested in other sections in this book, the trick is to find time to be alone with the person and then ask open-ended questions, never assuming that the new life-style is all roses and sunshine. Be aware that in some cases retirement or job loss may feel positive at first, but a few weeks or months later it can become devastating. Staying in touch over time, therefore, is important.

> Waking up with nothing special to do was nice for awhile, but it didn't last long. I realized how important it was for me to be producing something. I became almost frantic looking for something constructive to do.

> Retiree who later returned to work

If your friend or family member is willing to talk about the grief, the loneliness, the sense of inadequacy, by all means be supportive and listen to them. Let them know that allowing as much disclosure of negative feelings as needed, return the focus to accomplishments and achievements:

"What are you most proud of among your accomplishments?"

"Which parts of your work made you feel the best?"

"Do you think your wife/husband/children ever really understood what you did at work? You might think about telling them."

Help your friend or relative understand that it is normal and healthy to grieve the loss of job when work contributed so much to their self-image. It is also normal to be angry if one has been forced to leave a position which they handled competently.

I knew I had a lot of knowledge and it would have helped so much if I could at least have taught it to someone else. But no one wanted what I had to offer.

Retiree

Besides being a supportive listener, there are several practical things you can do to help. Suggest that letters of support and commendation be obtained from the ex-employer, if at all possible. These are very valuable in seeking other employment and in applying for volunteer work. Putting together a portfolio of major accomplishments helps one focus on the positive and provides an excellent support tool for looking for other work.

If your friend is eager to work again, either for gainful employment or as a volunteer, help search for positions. Keep your contacts open for leads and check the want ads. Many not-for-profit agencies and programs utilize volunteers just like they do employees with applications, interviews, training, supervision, and evaluations.

Be aware of new financial restraints when planning social events. It is patronizing to plan an expensive outing and offer to pay his or her way. Rather than humiliating your friend or family member, it is far better to plan inexpensive activities.

If paying basic bills becomes a problem and you have the resources, it is appropriate to offer to help out with a loan. Only the closest of friends or relatives will be willing to accept money as a gift, and even then it may be embarrassing. Loans help keep personal integrity in tact. If you truly wish not to be repaid, suggest that the repayment money be used to help someone else who needs it.

As you spend time with this person, explore ways that his or her talent, education, and expertise can still be put to good use. Teachers can tutor or substitute teach. Ministers can conduct workshops or do part-time work at smaller churches. Retired executives can offer their expertise to various agencies on a consultant basis.

Volunteer work can't be overemphasized. Some people consider writing articles or books about their work. Others find pleasure in doing something entirely different, such as working as a school crossing guard, rocking babies in the neonatal nursery of a hospital, or selling peanuts at the stadium. The foster-grandparents program is a wonderful way to stay in touch with children. With the right qualifications and good parenting skills, providing a home to a foster child can be rewarding and bring in some income as well.

Most important of all, stay in touch and ask how it's going. Most people will not bring up the subject of the retirement or the job loss if they sense humiliation and embarrassment. Understand the need to express those "less up-beat" feelings. Offer your concern and support regularly.

Forced Retirement

If you sense that the person is continuing down a depressive spiral or seems to be stuck in an angry or resentful position, suggest professional counseling. Point out that you understand that loss of meaningful work involves a difficult grieving process and that you no longer believe that your support is adequate. Make the suggestion a couple of times, and if the advice is not taken, drop it. However, if the depression seems to reach a suicidal state, refer to the information on suicide in Chapter 19 of this book and insist that professional help be obtained.

CHAPTER ELEVEN

PROPERTY LOSS

Theft or burglary can be immensely frightening and unsettling. It can be so personal that it makes people feel violated, even though their bodies were never touched. Some have said that burglary can be more disturbing than a robbery because of the lack of identity of the offender. Every face on the street becomes the burglar.

Theft and burglary, even in the form of a purse-snatching, hold special significance for the elderly, handicapped, or others who are especially vulnerable. A high percentage of unanticipated deaths follow victimization of these populations. Some speculate that the fear and defenselessness they feel is partially responsible.

People's "belongings" are a part of who they are. To have one's clothing rummaged through by an intruder, sentimental pieces of jewelry taken, papers ripped from a desk or file, or family silver and china taken, means more than the monetary value of the property. In addition, there is the fear that if it happened once, it can happen again. It is normal and appropriate to deeply grieve these losses.

Nothing prepares one for the experience of having their belongings suddenly taken. It is disorienting. Nearly all victims of theft report feeling out of control as they come to grips with the facts. People are often in a mild state of shock before they acknowledge that they have become crime victims. At first, they can't think what to do, who to tell. Simply listing the items missing and contacting the police can take a long time. Just as they were helpless in preventing what happened, they continue to feel helpless in doing anything about it.

As a helpful friend or family member, offer emotional support first. The initial response of family, friends, and law enforcement officers has much to do with the emotional outcome of the victim. Becoming impatient or angry with a victim only adds to the emotional trauma. Above all, don't blame the victim with questions such as:

"Why didn't you have better locks?"

"Why wasn't the window closed?"

"Why were you carrying that much money?"

"Why didn't you carry adequate insurance?"

"Why don't you calm down and act like an adult?"

"I can't believe you can't remember what he looked like."

He or she will feel guilty enough without someone else asking the same questions that they will ask themselves many times.

If the police have not been called when you arrive, suggest that the call be made, or do it yourself, before anything is touched. Let the investigating officer ask all the factual questions. Your role is to express your sorrow that it happened and offer concrete help, not to question.

Understand that because of shock, it may be difficult for the victim to think how to answer the questions of the investigator. Offer your assistance if needed. After the law enforcement officers have completed their initial investigation, help clean up the mess. Be aware that everything disturbed now will feel tainted to the victim. Just knowing that the burglar touched everything that is now in disarray will be emotionally upsetting. Victims are often especially troubled by disdainful behaviors on the part of the burglar, such as smoldering cigarette butts, food eaten from the refrigerator, and the use of bathroom facilities.

Try to understand how frightening such an experience can be. Plan to spend time with the victim, particularly at night and during the time of day when the theft or robbery took place. Extend an invitation to sleep at your home for awhile. Offer your help in changing and securing locks, doors, and windows. Do everything possible to make the home as secure as possible. Encourage the victim to write down any pieces of information he or she forgot to tell the investigator and report it. Offer to help with tasks which may seem overwhelming to the victim, such as contacting insurance companies and credit card companies.

If a suspect was observed and is arrested, offer to accompany your friend or family member to the line-up. This, too, can be a frightening and anxiety-producing experience for the victim.

Above all, offer the opportunity for the victim to continue talking about what happened. Know that he or she is not "all right" even before you ask and, therefore approach the subject with a question like, "Well, how scared are you today?" or "Is it any better for you today than it was yesterday?" Let them tell the story as often as they want. Retelling the story is a way of regaining control.

I still have nightmares about someone coming in.
Every time I hear a noise, I almost freeze in fear.

Victim of a robbery

It is as true for children as adults that the best way to overcome fear is to express it. All too often children are told to, "Just go on and forget about it." They can't forget about it any more than the adults can! It is important for them to express their fears and receive support from the adults that every precaution possible has been taken to prevent a recurrence. Provide keys for the children so they can check locked doors. This helps them take control. Don't be surprised if nightmares become a problem. Children need emotional support and the opportunity to talk about fears and anxieties while being touched or held by the parent.

If the burglar is caught (most aren't) the victim may have to face the offender not only at a line-up but during the trial. This can be upsetting. It can be especially so if hate violence (violence based on race, religion, or sexual orientation) was involved in the destruction of the property. Plan to accompany your friend or family member to court, and offer to drive them home. If the offender is acquitted, or found guilty but later released from his sentence, be prepared to help make your friend or family member feel as safe as possible. Unfortunately for the victim, this may mean moving, obtaining an unlisted phone number, and taking other security measures which are frustrating and humiliating. It is bad enough to lose one's belongings with personal meaning. It is even worse to realize the criminal can arouse fear and anxiety for a long time.

PART III

HELPING PRINCIPLES

CHAPTER TWELVE

EMPATHETIC LISTENING

Even though the person you want to help falls into one of the ten "Specific Situations" just listed, there are some general principles for helping those suffering from any kind of loss. That is what this Chapter is about.

When hundreds of people recovering from loss or pain were asked, "What helps?" their responses came down to the following:

o   Being allowed to talk about it when I wanted to

o   Having all my feelings accepted

o   Being with others who have had a similar experience.[1]

Those three statements are simple enough. But are they really that simple? For most of us, it is very difficult to help our hurting friend or family member in these ways.

It's difficult because we don't like being around people in pain. When they hurt, we hurt. It's more fun to be with people who make us feel good.

Having the patience to listen and accept what we hear is also difficult, because what we really want is to make them feel better so we can feel better. That seems more heroic.

Your goal is not to make your friend or relative "hurry through their pain," or even to feel better, but to convey the fact that you care and are willing to share in the suffering. Suffering is a normal response to loss, no matter what the loss may be. Accepting reality and sharing honest, open communication means so much more than acting like nothing has happened.

> After we realized that she was probably going to die, I treasured those few friends who talked honestly with us about how they were feeling. The kids said the same thing. Some of them talked with friends. Some of them talked with their aunt. We treasure the ones who were honest with us, because it made it easier for us to be honest with them.
>
> Husband whose wife later
> died of cancer

It is necessary to feel the loss deeply for awhile. Attempts to prematurely lift a person out of the pain can be resented and rejected.

I wondered why people kept doing this and that and telling me it would 'make me feel better.' Nothing would make me feel better, and I didn't even want to feel better.

Young wife whose husband was killed in a vehicular crash

When someone is suffering a loss, the only real remedy is to restore the someone or something that has been lost. Unfortunately, you can't do that. But minimizing that loss or suggesting alternatives won't work. Yearning to have the lost person, relationship or situation restored is absolutely normal. Since you <u>can't</u> make things the way they were before, you are of greatest service if you simply support their suffering, rather than try to "make it better."

Of all the people who came to the house the day our son died, I remember only one. When I opened the door, there was my neighbor. He didn't say a word, but he embraced me and wept with me. What a blessing he was.

Father whose son was killed by a drunk driver

Within the first few days I was told by several people that I was young and would remarry, that I was spared by God for some reason, and that the accident was God's will and I would have to accept it.

Woman whose husband and two children were killed in a vehicular crash. She had 15 broken bones and serious internal injuries

There are some effective ways to help or comfort, but first let's discuss some tactics which don't help. Following is a list of phrases which people often say but prove unhelpful because they minimize the situation:

"Everything's going to be okay."

"It must be God's will."

"You're lucky you weren't hurt more seriously."

"Just be thankful she's alive."

"You're lucky to have other fine children."

"You're young. You'll find someone else."

"It would have been worse if........"

"Luckily, there aren't any children."

"You're looking great!" (when they don't)

"You're so strong." (They probably don't feel strong and will resent it if they think you expect them to be strong. It is a burden to have to be an "inspiration.")

"Are you feeling better yet?" (Implies a needed "yes" response.)

Chapter Twelve and Chapter Thirteen of this book are about eight principles which will help you to appropriately meet the needs of someone you care about who is hurting. The principles are divided into two groups; the Empathetic Listening Chapter and the Active Support Chapter. The first covers four principles relating to empathetic listening. While sympathy means feeling "for" another, empathy means feeling

Helping Principles

"with" another. It means you are willing to hurt too. The four principles within the Active Support Chapter are concerned with actions you can take to help someone.

You may find yourself reading material already covered in one of the "Specific Situations." That's because these principles are generic and helpful in all situations. Hopefully, you'll benefit from refreshing your memory and integrating the new specific material with the old.

While the specifics may vary from case to case, these suggestions will work with most people in the following categories:

o   The physically injured

o   The seriously or terminally ill

o   The survivor whose loved one has died

o   The survivor whose loved one has been suddenly killed

o   The emotionally injured (rape, emotional abuse, theft, burglary, difficult retirement, loss of a valued job)

o   The separated (divorce, break-up of a love relationship, empty nest).

As you consider these suggested principles, think carefully about your friend or family member, then choose the techniques you think will work for both of you. They are not set in stone but are guides to help you think creatively about how best to be helpful. The first helping principle in Empathetic Listening is to learn that a good listener does just that--listens.

LISTENING

Listening is crucial in comforting others. It is not helpful to talk trivia or keep the conversation light so your friend or family member won't think about the pain in their life. Nor should you talk business or give advice when your friend is suffering from a breaking heart.

> People were too 'wordy.' They kept giving me advice and spouting off religious jargon. Their mere presence was meaningful to me, but not their words.
>
> Woman whose child was killed

Learn to listen. Really listen. Be comfortable with silences and crying.

> I cried every day for over a month. I have one friend who will always be with me when I need to cry and talk. She doesn't try to stop me. That means a lot.
>
> Mother whose daughter and her fiancee were killed by a drunk driver

People in pain need to talk about it in their own time. Almost all suffering people eventually want to tell the story of what happened to them. For example, if a loved one is now gone, the person left needs to talk about that person, sometimes putting the person on a pedestal for awhile. It is a way of assuring that the loved one won't be forgotten.

Listening

I felt a compulsion to tell everyone what had happened to me. I told the story again and again, matter-of-factly as if it were a dream or a movie script. The repetition made it real. In my mind I imagined the actual shooting over and over, trying to convince myself that it had really happened.

> Woman who survived a shooting in
> which three of her friends were killed

Most friends and relatives, however, tire of listening. If your goal is to be helpful and supportive, you must be willing to hear the story over and over, reflect on what you have heard, and ask questions to enable more full expression. As people talk about what happened and how they feel, they often discover solutions to problems that seemed insurmountable when kept inside.

While listening, be cautious about asking for too much disclosure, especially if what has happened is traumatic. Trauma can best be handled in small and intermittent doses. If your friend trusts you and knows you are available to listen when needed, more will be revealed in time. Don't push too hard.

> For several weeks after the crash, I couldn't talk about the gory details. Yet it seemed that was all anyone else was interested in. About a month after the crash, I needed to talk about the details, but by then all my friends were pretending nothing had happened.

> Woman whose family members
> were killed in a vehicular crash

HELPFUL COMMENTS:

Initial response:

> "I'm so sorry."

> "I can't imagine how difficult this is for you. With your permission, I'd like to be with you for awhile."

> "I'd give anything to be able to make it better for you, but I know I can't. Just know that I love you."

Later:

> "How are you feeling today?" (This works much better than "How are you?" which causes most people to automatically respond, "Fine.")

> "I was thinking about you and wondered what kind of a day you were having."

> "Do you feel like talking about it today?" Respect the answer.

> "Tell me about _____."

> "What is it like without him/her?"

> "How are you coping?"

> "Does it hurt more physically or emotionally?"

> "What is it like when _____?"

Use their words, not yours, at first. For example, "murder," "rape," and "sodomy," are very difficult to assimilate for victims of those crimes. "Death" and "divorce" are

Listening

words many people simply can't say for awhile. In time, these words can be helpful because giving what happened a "name" helps one begin to accept reality. Be aware of timing.

APPROPRIATE SUPPORT:

o   Call first to see if your friend or family member would like to be with you for awhile. If so, arrange for a time when the two of you can be alone.

o   Learn to be comfortable with silences and with crying. If you feel you must interject, say something like, "It's hard for you to talk about it...Just take your time" or "It's not easy to talk about this. I'll stick with you."

o   Cry with your friend or family member if it comes naturally. However, don't let your own devastation overshadow theirs. If you do that, you become the one in need of comfort, and that is not fair. It's a question of putting your friend's need above your own.

o   Reminisce about the "good times" and continue to refer to the missing person by name.

o   Be especially attentive in social settings. You can be assured that many others will avoid your friend in social settings because they won't want to face the unpleasant topic or because they don't know what to say.

CAUTIONS:

o   Don't force or suppress expression. Instead, encourage and enable it by asking open ended questions, and giving empathetic responses without false or premature reassurance. Reassurance offered too soon can be a conversation stopper no matter how well-intended.

o   Don't be in a hurry.

o   Don't waste time on trivia after the first few minutes. "Well, how are you?" is an excellent bridging phrase.

o   Don't interrupt silence unless you can improve on it.

Listening

When I ask you to listen to me
    and you start giving advice,
    you have not done what I asked.

When I ask you to listen to me
    and you begin to tell me why I shouldn't feel
    that way, you are trampling on <u>my</u> feelings.

When I ask you to listen to me and you feel you have
    to <u>do</u> something to solve my problem you have
    failed me, strange as that may seem.

Listen! All I asked was that you listen--
    not talk or do. Just hear me.

Advice is cheap. A quarter will get you both Dear
    Abby and Billy Graham in the same newspaper.

And I can <u>do</u> for myself. I'm not helpless.
    Maybe discouraged and faltering, but not
    helpless.

When you do something for me
    that I can and need to do for myself,
    you contribute to my fear and inadequacy.

But when you accept as a simple fact
    that I do feel what I feel, no matter how
    irrational, then I can quit trying to convince you
    and can get about the business of
    understanding what's behind this irrational
    feeling.

And when that's clear,
    the answers are obvious
    and I don't need advice.

Irrational feelings make sense
    when we understand what's behind them.

Perhaps that's why prayer works,
    sometimes, for some people--
    because God is mute
    and He/She doesn't give advice or try to fix
    things.

So please listen and just hear me.
    And if you want to talk,
    wait a minute for your turn,
    and I'll listen to you.

        Ralph Roughton, M.D.

COPING WITH INTENSE EMOTIONS

Most of us grew up with the oft-repeated phrase, "You shouldn't feel that way." We learned that we shouldn't get angry, feel jealous, or succumb to despair, bitterness, hate, rage, or vengeance.

What a folly! Did it work when you were told not to feel a certain way? Of course not. In an effort to comply, however, you may have stopped being so vocal about your feelings and crammed them down inside.

Your willingness now to affirm your friendship with free expression of feelings is extremely therapeutic. It is a kind of validation that one needs when going through a vulnerable period. The full range of emotions that human beings can experience exists for a purpose. It is appropriate to be enraged when someone loved has been senselessly killed.

One jerk had the gall to tell me he knew what I was going through because he had recently buried his 99-year-old uncle. My young son had been suddenly killed. I can't tell you how furious that made me.

Father whose son was killed by a drunk driver

No one, not even my husband, understood my murderous rage. I turned on all the faucets in the bathroom to scream.

Mother whose son was murdered

It is appropriate to despair in trying to restore equilibrium after someone who was regularly depended on has died. It is appropriate to be exceedingly glad to be alive after surviving a rape, an assault, or a serious illness or injury--and feel intermittently vengeful anger about it.

> A rush of relief flooded over me. 'I'm alive! I'm alive! I'm alive!' raced through my mind. I was deeply, undeniably, wondrously happy to be there in that stark white hospital gown.
>
> Stabbing victim

> My family and friends seemed terribly upset about what had happened to me, and I was too. But I was also almost euphoric. I was so glad to still be alive that I literally celebrated every breath.
>
> Rape victim

Most people get very uncomfortable when someone expresses intensely negative feelings. They may fear that beyond the feelings lurk irrational thinking and the potential for destructive behaviors.

If you sense that irrational thinking or planning is creeping in, question the pros and cons of the thought. Try to assess the situation realistically. Look at proposed behaviors and help your friend or relative consider both the positive and negative consequences of implementing the plans. Search together for alternatives which will be less destructive.

Usually, though, the freedom to ventilate feelings is all that is needed.

When her step-sister got there, she became completely hysterical. A friend told her, 'Stop the hysterics! The family doesn't need that now.' That troubled me. I felt she had a right to be hysterical and to grieve however she needed to--I eventually told my friend exactly how I felt.

Mother whose daughter was
murdered by her boyfriend

Fantasies about what one would like to have happen to the person responsible for the pain are fine, especially if they are shared. They are a constructive way of expressing feelings. Very often sharing these fantasies results in laughter and a release of tension. As your friend shares feelings and fantasies with you, together you can discover how to resolve some of the pain or to express it in a safe way.

HELPFUL COMMENTS:

"Please don't be upset about crying in front of me. It's normal for you to cry. I'd be worried about you if you didn't."

"If I were in your shoes, I imagine I would feel the same way."

"It sounds to me like you feel name the emotion ." (Labeling an emotion gives a sense of control over it.)

HURTFUL COMMENTS:

"You shouldn't feel that way."

"I can't believe you're saying that."

"Forget about it. You've got to get on with your life."

"Let's not talk about that."

"Feeling that way won't help a thing."

"Your anguish won't bring him/her back, so forget it."

"It couldn't be that bad."

"You're actually lucky. It would have been worse if..."

APPROPRIATE SUPPORT:

o   Spend some time processing your own feelings about what has happened. Remember not to tell yourself you "shouldn't feel ___."

o   Encourage your friend to cry and to sigh. These two behaviors release tension and anxiety. Being sad is preferable to being anxious and tense.

o   Encourage expressions of anger that are not destructive, such as hitting pillows, throwing ice cubes at brick walls, running, yelling, or cursing in a private place.

o   If your friend expresses a lot of feelings, call the next day to say how much it meant to you that he or she chose to be so open with you. This will eliminate any fear that too much was revealed.

o   Encourage your friend to write a letter to the person responsible for the pain and explain in detail the outcome of what has happened. Discuss the pros and cons of actually mailing it.

CAUTIONS:

o   Don't encourage your friend or family member to express their negative intense emotions to people who could be expected to retaliate with hostility.

o   Don't let the intense feelings of your friend or family member frighten you off. You are needed now more than ever.

o   Don't become so engrossed in the pain of your friend or family member that you get depressed or overwhelmed. Continue to spend time, maybe even more than usual, with other friends who are in good spirits and who care about you.

o   Don't betray confidentiality. If your friend or family member trusted you enough to be honest and open with you, you must not betray that trust by telling others. The consequences will be embarrassment and retracted trust.

DEALING WITH GUILT

Guilt is very often the most difficult component of suffering to overcome because of the ease with which others place blame.

Several people said, 'If he had had a seat-belt on, he probably would have lived.' That may be true, but it broke my heart to hear them say it.

Mother whose son was killed
by a drunk driver

People kept telling me that if I had just worked less and spent more time at home, she wouldn't have left me.

Separating Husband

It is frightening to know that suffering may be lurking just around the corner and that we are all vulnerable to it.

My husband was killed shortly after we moved to Chicago. Several people blamed me for moving the family to that area.

Wife whose husband was killed while
riding a motorcycle

It is devastating to think that someone deliberately chose to hurt us or someone we love. Therefore, largely on a subconscious level, people often blame themselves. Then, at least, what has happened makes some sense. Life doesn't feel so out of control.

Dealing With Guilt

Your friend or family member may go to great lengths to find ways to feel guilty. That is normal in the beginning. If unrealistic guilt persists over time, it can destroy the person experiencing it.

Eventually, blame will need to be placed realistically. A portion of what happened may, indeed, be his or her fault. That part should be acknowledged and, if possible, forgiven. No one is perfect. People usually make the best choices possible at the time of a crisis. Sometimes they are not the right choices.

In most cases, the person suffering did nothing to ask for it. Giving up the search for the elusive "why" is a major step forward.

'Why did this happen to me?' I pleaded after realizing the extent of my injuries.

'Just because it did,' my therapist responded. 'You didn't ask for it. You didn't deserve it. But it happened. So let's go on from here and not try to answer questions that have no answers.'

That helped.

Victim of vehicular crash
with serious leg injury

HELPFUL COMMENTS:

At First:

"It's not your fault." (Never assess blame early on. It can be considered later.)

Later:

"When were you first aware of what was happening?"

"Was there any way you could have known what would happen?"

"What could you have known or done in order to prevent it?

"Tell me as much as you know about what happened."

"Would she want you to carry all this guilt?"

Discussing these questions will help identify the components over which your friend or family member had no control.

INAPPROPRIATE COMMENTS:

"Why did you/didn't you _____?"

"If only you had _____."

"Why were you _____?"

APPROPRIATE SUPPORT:

o   Help your friend or family member obtain the facts about what happened. Only as the facts are known can blame be appropriately placed. Help obtain medical reports and autopsy reports. Go to the library and research illnesses or injuries. If a crime was committed, suggest obtaining a copy of the crime report. Talk to the investigating officer and prosecutor. Your friend or relative might hire a private investigator, if financially possible and many unanswered questions persist.

o   If your friend or family member was to blame at all, try to help pinpoint the amount of blame it is realistic to carry. Along with that, offer the suggestion that at the time, those involved made the best decisions they knew how to make and would never have chosen for this to happen.

o   Consider avenues of seeking justice for the part of the trauma that was someone else's fault. This may mean filing criminal charges or instigating civil litigation.

CAUTIONS:

o   Don't underestimate the power of guilt, especially survivor guilt, to devastate. When others have been killed or injured, those who survive may feel terribly guilty simply because they survived. Tackling survivor guilt may require professional help.

o   Don't reinforce illegitimate feelings of guilt in your conversation.

SHARING YOUR OWN EXPERIENCES

Focusing on someone else's pain has a mysterious way of refocusing us on ours. It can trigger unresolved grieving and plunge us into a compulsion to talk about our own experiences. Unfortunately, the next step is often saying, "I know exactly how you feel."

"I know how you feel" is the most resented phrase of all the platitudes shared with persons in pain. "It was God's will" runs a close second. Resentment increases if the well-wisher goes on to explain <u>why</u> he knows how the other feels. No two people's experiences are exactly the same. Even if they are similar, it is presumptuous to think that one person knows exactly how another feels.

> People kept telling me they knew how I felt, and how much they missed their dog or their grandmother. One lady talked on and on about losing her baby to crib death. I know all those things hurt, but I couldn't see that their experiences even began to compare with mine.
>
> Mother whose child was killed

If you have had a truly similar experience, it is very helpful for you to say so. It will enhance trust and credibility. But that is enough.

> I helped a neighbor last year when his daughter was killed. In a room full of people, he called out to me and said I was the only one there who knew how he felt because I, too, had lost a child.
>
> Women whose son was killed

Sharing Experiences

Your role now is to enable your friend or family member to lean into their own pain and ventilate their feelings about it. Difficult as it may be, you must restrain yourself from going into your own pain in detail.

> From the moment my family arrived, I felt even worse. They were so distraught I couldn't get a word in edgewise. Rather than listening to me, they wept and moaned about their own distress.
>
> Assault victim

As time goes on, you will be <u>asked</u> about your experiences as your friend or family member tries to understand what has happened to them. This will be the time, not before, to share your story.

The issue of shared grieving is an extremely difficult one for families. It is crushing for spouses, parents, and children to observe the pain of one they love so much. And yet, the last thing the primary sufferer needs is the added stress of witnessing the pain and anxiety of those he loves. It can cause him to decide to suppress his own feelings in order to attend to theirs. Those nearest and dearest need to walk the fine line between hearing and accepting the pain of the sufferer, and offering hope and optimism. If you want to support your friend or loved one, but find that you, too, are in need of support, seek it elsewhere.

HELPFUL COMMENTS:

If a Similar Loss:

> "My child, too, was killed."

> "I, also, was raped."

> "I, too, have lost a love."

"I felt something like that, too,
when _____."

If Not a Similar Loss

"I can't imagine how this must be for you."

"I feel for your pain."

INAPPROPRIATE COMMENTS:

"I know exactly how you feel."

"I fully understand."

APPROPRIATE SUPPORT:

o   Even if you are not close, but the experience is traumatic and common, you can be a valuable resource. For example, when a child is killed, it is rare that anyone else in his or her family or friendship circle has been likewise traumatized. Others whose child has been killed can initiate the contact by way of a handwritten note or very brief phone call explaining that something similar happened to them. They can offer to meet together if desired.

o   Discuss your story only when asked, and be honest. Too much self-revelation on your part risks diminishing the importance of your friend's experience.

CAUTIONS:

o   Don't expect your friend or family member to experience their trauma the same way you experienced yours. Even if the trauma is similar, you will experience it differently.

o   Don't compare your experiences. Comparing always feels like minimizing to the receiver.

CHAPTER THIRTEEN

ACTIVE SUPPORT

PROVIDING PRACTICAL ASSISTANCE

Now that we've dealt with how to listen empathetically, let's turn to some principles for providing support of a more concrete nature. The first section of this chapter suggests ways of providing practical assistance to someone. Sometimes those suffering a loss need some practical help so that they can focus all their attention on their recovery.

Ill or injured persons obviously cannot carry on maintenance of their families and homes. Neither can emotionally devastated people.

In spite of this knowledge, we often fear that stepping in to help will appear intrusive. We resolve our guilt by making the safe, but useless, statement, "Let me know if there's anything I can do."

Practical Assistance

A person in distress may not be able to think about what needs to be done, and is even less likely to be able to be assertive enough to ask for assistance.

> After I got home from the hospital, everyone assumed that unless I asked for help, I didn't need it. It's hard to not be able to do things, and it's also hard to keep asking.
>
> > Woman who suffered serious
> > internal injury and mild head injury
> > in a vehicular crash

The tradition of bringing in food is a good one. Until one goes through troubled times a person might think, "Why in the world do people put so much emphasis on food which has nothing to do with what has happened." When trouble comes, though, nearly all families are grateful for the food brought in, perhaps more for the symbolic gesture than for the actual value. (Deeply bereaved people are not hungry and don't like being told, "You must eat. It will make you feel better.")

> Ladies from the church brought in a hot meal every day for two weeks. I don't know how I would have made it without them, because I couldn't do anything but just exist.
>
> > Mother whose child was killed

As you think about the practical needs of your hurting friend or family member, be aware that simply getting through the day with the most basic of personal and home maintenance may be all that can be accomplished. If it's not too intrusive and it needs to be done, just do it. Close friends can enter one's home and assume maintenance responsibilities. More distant friends and acquaintances will need to explain specifically what they would like to do, and ask permission.

I am a single parent, so when I was taken to the hospital after the wreck, no one was available for the house or my children. A friend got my mail, took care of the kids, and ran the necessary errands for me. After I got home, I was still in a lot of pain and, because of a head injury, was very weak and forgetful. Two friends brought in some meals, cleaned the children's rooms, trimmed the bushes, and transported the kids, even to get school clothes.

Crash victim

However, no one should do more than the basics. Rearranging furniture and cleaning closets and drawers are too intrusive, and are resented.

HELPFUL COMMENTS:

"I don't imagine you've been able to do your housework, and I want so much to do something for you. May I send my cleaning person over to work for you one day this week?" (You can offer to do the cleaning yourself, but some people are embarrassed about their friends seeing their 'dirt.')

"May I keep your children on __(day)__?"

"I'd like to have you come over for lunch on __day__. Can you come?"

"I imagine Christmas will be hard for you this year. I'm going shopping on __(day)__ and if you'd give me a list of the people you need to buy for, and any ideas you have, I'd love to shop for you."

Practical Assistance

INAPPROPRIATE COMMENTS:

"Let me know if there's anything I can do."

"Call me if you need me."

APPROPRIATE SUPPORT:

You Don't Need to Ask to:

o   Water and mow the lawn.

o   Take in a dish of food, preferably something that can be frozen if not needed immediately.

o   Give a gift.

o   Donate blood for the ill or injured.

o   Contribute to a cause which is meaningful to your friend or family member. Ask the organization to acknowledge the gift to them.

Ask First:

o   Offer to stay at the home and take phone calls, receive food and guests (following death or during hospitalization).

o   Offer child care on a specific date.

o   Offer to care for pets.

o   Offer transportation.

o   Offer to take vehicles for gas, oil check, etc.

o   Offer your professional skills.

o   Offer to address thank-you notes.

o   Offer to inform employer or school, social security, insurance companies, creditors, bank, cancel subscriptions, etc., following a death.

o   Offer money (If a monetary gift is too humiliating, offer a loan).

CAUTIONS:

o   Don't be intrusive inside a person's home without asking first, unless you are very close.

o   Don't remove clothing and "things" of a deceased person from the house. That task is best done by the "nearest and dearest" when they are ready to do it.

o   Don't insist on anything if a person says "no."

SENDING NOTES

Never underestimate the power of the written word. A note doesn't require a response. Notes can be read time and time again.

Notes and letters meant so much. I had no idea how many people cared that much.

Woman whose husband was
terminally ill

After he was killed, I got several notes from his teachers and friends telling us what a kind boy he was, how polite he was, and how much he meant to them. I will always treasure those.

Mother whose son was killed

A written word of care and concern means so much, especially after time has passed, and everyone else seems to have forgotten what happened.

A friend sent me flowers and a note on my son's birthday. I just knew I was the only one remembering that it would have been his birthday. That meant all the world to me.

Mother whose son was murdered

It is amazing how our society expects us to "go on, business as usual" with little, if any, understanding of the emotional trauma of the hurting experience.

Suddenly, after a week or two, no one called, or sent a note, or even acted like anything had happened. If anybody said anything, it was something like, 'You just have to put this behind you now.'

Mother whose daughter was killed

Holidays are always difficult for people in pain. Television and magazine advertisements are filled with happy, intact families celebrating together. What a dramatic contrast to the experience of the lonely and hurting.

On Mother's Day, I had all the kids over and we spent the afternoon going through photos and reminiscing. It was good for us all. I can't imagine how that first Mother's Day without a mother (and a wife) would have been for us all if we had tried to go through the day 'business as usual.'

Husband whose wife died of cancer

Birthdays, too, can be devastating if the special person one is used to celebrating with is no longer present.

My dear and wise friend invited me to spend the entire day at her house on the date that would have been his first birthday. She knew I couldn't cope with that day by myself.

Mother whose infant died

Wedding anniversaries are painful for the unhappily divorced or divorcing.

The anniversary of death dates, especially for survivors of a sudden, violent death, are extremely difficult. Pain associated with those dates is so frequently reported that it has been labeled "anniversary syndrome."

> It's been a year since it happened, and I feel like I'm reliving it all over again. I've been having nightmares, and a lot of the old fears have returned. I'm dreading the actual anniversary day. I doubt if anyone else will remember. I'm not sure how I'm going to spend it, but I'm sure I will hurt a lot.
>
> Wife whose husband was killed

Anniversary syndrome not only involves the actual anniversary date, but the weeks preceding it. Survivors dread it and can become depressed for weeks leading into it.

Even the season of the year can trigger unpleasant memories. If a loved one was hospitalized or died in January, the sight of barren trees and brown grass or the feel of cold wintry wind can bring back potent images of the loss as well as the feelings which accompanied it. Rape or assault victims, or those whose spouse or lover has left them, often feel such recurring pain, too.

It feels very special to be remembered at these times.

WHAT TO WRITE:

Please see Appendix for Sample Notes. Following is a very helpful note.

> This week of your mother's death has been one of many emotions for me. It has brought back so many memories. I've been thinking of all the good times you and Sheryl used to have and how much she enjoyed going out to the farm. She admired your parents so much, and I have always felt that

they helped so much in her 'growing up' process.
I'm sure I didn't let your parents know how much
I appreciated all that they did for her and that I
couldn't have picked better friends for her. I shall
miss your mother. You are loved.

Woman writing to her daughter's
friend whose mother died

APPROPRIATE SUPPORT:

o   Try to get in touch with what you would like to
    say but are afraid you might not be able to say in
    person. Say it in a note.

o   Send flowers or a book with a personal note on
    birthdates, deathdates, or other special days. It is
    especially important to remember anniversary time.

o   If someone has died, write down special memories
    of the person and send them to the family. This is
    especially meaningful for children who have lost a
    classmate. It is a very therapeutic exercise for
    them, and the memories will be treasured by the
    family.

HANDLING SECOND VICTIMIZATIONS

Experiencing trauma is not an isolated event. It usually involves coping with many additional hurts, often referred to as "second victimizations" or "second injuries." Examples follow.

> Instead of helping me get back to work, I was told to write a letter of resignation. Being nice, I wrote the letter. Later I learned that by doing that, I had terminated all my rights to financial assistance from my job.
>
> > Woman whose child was killed and who had difficulty concentrating at work

> An insurance adjustor sneaked into ICU to try to get me to sign release papers.
>
> > Injured woman

> When I got to the funeral home, a very condescending young man in hushed tones tried to sell me as much as he could. At first he showed me only two kinds of caskets and then started talking about my need to buy a double plot. When I explained that I didn't know where I might be when I died, he tried to put a guilt trip on me about being buried next to my wife.
>
> > Husband whose wife had died

I was lying in the hospital with a bullet hole in my back when I got a letter from the Victim Compensation Program that 'information submitted is insufficient to establish that you sustained an injury on the above-shown date.'

Shooting victim

Suddenly my in-laws seemed to want me totally out of the picture. All they seemed interested in was getting my husband's money and estate.

Woman whose husband was killed
by a drunk driver

They showed it over and over on TV. Why did they do that? Everyone told me they'd seen it. I didn't want them to talk about it and be so curious.

Teen whose last living parent was
killed in a freak accident

I had waited and waited, praying that he would live. Suddenly, a young intern, blood still on his shirt, came in, hopped upon a gurney and said, 'Your son has expired.' That's all. He then turned and left me there.

Woman whose son was stabbed
in the heart at a high school
graduation party

> I couldn't believe my parents invited a reporter
> and photographers into my hospital room. I didn't
> want anyone to see me. Now my attackers know
> I'm still alive.
>
> Woman who was gang raped

While it is very rare for these people to intentionally inflict pain on someone who is hurting, it is an all-too-common reality. Persons in pain already feel vulnerable, powerless, and often fearful. They feel they no longer have control over their own lives.

As others counted on for help not only fail to be helpful, but are hurtful, that sense of vulnerability and powerlessness is enhanced. Added to the primary loss, it can be overwhelming. If you want to be genuinely helpful, you need to be as available to listen and offer support through the "second victimizations" as you were when the crisis first occurred. You may also need to intervene with oppressive persons or systems as an advocate for your friend or family member.

HELPFUL COMMENTS:

> "I'm so sorry you have to cope with that, too. It's
> not your fault and it makes me sad and mad."
>
> "Let's see if we can figure out what can be done
> about this."
>
> "Would you like for me to go with you to talk with
> _____?" (This is especially appreciated
> in coping with powerful organizations or systems.)

INAPPROPRIATE COMMENTS:

> "Don't worry about it. You're getting better is all that matters."

> "Just blow it off. You've got enough to think about already."

> "I don't know anything about that." (You can learn!)

APPROPRIATE SUPPORT:

o Be willing to listen empathetically to stories of second victimizations the same way you listened to the primary story.

o Ask your friend or family member if they would like you to seek information on their behalf.

With Permission:

o If legal action is involved, go to a law library and ask for a copy of the laws affecting the situation.

o Go to a medical school library to seek information about illnesses or injuries.

o Call the State Commission on Insurance and ask about appropriate insurance policy and procedures (get the phone number from the State Capitol switchboard).

o Obtain information from programs which provide services to persons experiencing specific losses. Local crisis hotlines or Mental Health Associations can inform you of these programs and their location. Support groups of persons experiencing similar losses are immensely therapeutic.

o   If your friend or family member's social network fails, help establish a new one. This means inviting them to new places where they can meet new people.

CAUTIONS:

o   Don't attempt to handle second victimizations <u>for</u> your friend or relative unless he or she are totally powerless and devastated. Instead, enable and assist. Work on it together.

o   Don't assume that you know what's best and act accordingly. Always ask.

GIVING GIFTS

A gift can say a thousand words. Flowers say "I care about you," no matter when they're sent. If you are talented in writing, an original saying of framed calligraphy shows both talent and time in offering yourself personally. Books not only say that you care, but can be very helpful. A small piece of art bearing a particular message can become a treasure. Records or tapes can be enjoyed again and again.

I'll never forget the single rose floating in a snifter with a card saying 'from all the kindergarten children you taught in twenty years of Sunday School.' What a wonderful way to remember.

Daughter of father who died

A gesture that encourages your friend or family member to express their thoughts in writing may be the greatest gift you can offer. A journal or diary can open the door to their self-expression and healing.

When writing in an open and relaxed state, people write things that they would never say. Writing can uncover lost or repressed feelings which need expression.

After the abortion, my mother suggested that I write three letters: one to my unborn baby, one to the father of the baby, and one to myself. I was surprised to learn how deep my feelings about it were.

Daughter following abortion

In the process of writing, often tears will come. The written words behind these tears, can provide valuable insights. Through crying, people can touch parts of themselves never revealed in any other way.

Teenagers, especially, seem to value writing. They, more than any other age group, feel embarrassed about revealing their emotions, especially crying in public. Because they want to express themselves, however, writing is an acceptable outlet.

Writing also provides a tool for measuring progress in recovery. It helps to look at what one wrote three months ago or six months ago and compare it with the present.

It is not unusual for people who write to want to share some of their writings. While it would be intrusive to specifically ask to read them, you can tell your friend or family member that you'd love to read any of their writings when they are ready to share them. Sometimes the writings lead to valuable contributions to fellow sufferers.

> I sometimes cautiously share the long letter I wrote my father the morning of his funeral, when they are farther along in grieving. That letter re-opens my grief, but builds a bridge of vulnerability that helps others accept their grieving too.
>
> Daughter of heart attack victim

> I was a communications major when I decided to get out of my battering relationship. Starting with what I had written during those years, I did my master's thesis on battered women and how they are depicted in the media.
>
> Battered woman who left her relationship

HELPFUL COMMENTS:

"I want you to have this because _____."

"I thought of you when I saw this_____."

"Some people find it helpful to write about what they're going through. It doesn't change anything, but it can help process what's happening. So I bought you this journal/diary."

"If you ever write anything you decide to share, I'd love to read it."

"I thought you'd like this picture of_____. You may not have seen it before."

APPROPRIATE SUPPORT:

o   Think about the special hurt your friend or family member is experiencing and plan your gift accordingly.

o   Find poems or pieces others have written when experiencing a similar loss. Clip or copy them for your friend or family member.

CAUTIONS:

o   Don't underline in books to be given as gifts.

o   Don't insist that a person write if they don't like to. If you think self expression would help, a tape recorder is another option.

o   Don't expect immediate gratitude for your gift. Some people deeply in distress will be appreciative, but will not have the energy to let you know until some time later.

o   Don't ask later if they read what you gave them. They may not have, or may not have found it helpful. Your caring act is what's important.

Part IV

SPECIAL ISSUES

CHAPTER FOURTEEN

UNDERSTANDING THE
REACTIONS OF CHILDREN

When I was about six, both my grandmother and my favorite Sunday School teacher died. Because my grandmother was very old and had been in a nursing home, I didn't know her well, so I didn't grieve much. However, it upset me a lot to see my parents, aunts, and uncles grieving so hard. I knew my Sunday School teacher much better. I touched her body in the casket and remember how cold and stiff and 'waxy' she felt. She was so white. I cried and missed her. When I was in the 4th grade, a little boy in our school got run over and killed. His body had been taken away by the time I got out, but I remember stepping over his blood in the street. When my mother heard about it, she got hysterical. No one in my family talked to me about life and death or about what I was feeling when any of these deaths happened.

> Woman writing of her first
> experience with death

It is senseless to try to protect children from pain within a family. Most children are more perceptive than adults about sensing that something is wrong. They pick up on facial expressions and overhear conversations. They are aware of changed schedules and new and different people coming and going. A child who sees adults crying, tense, impatient, and tired, but is told that nothing is wrong, feels confused, alienated and betrayed.

They said Grandma just went away for awhile. I didn't know why she never came back. Didn't she love us any more?

Women remembering her
reaction at age six

It is natural for adults to want to protect their children from pain. That, however, is impossible. Therefore, it is best to keep the children informed and allow them to express their fears and sorrows about what is happening. As the child experiences the adults in his life being sad, he learns that it is acceptable for him to be sad, too. Sharing these experiences together will help children learn that painful and unfair things do happen in life, but people can survive them.

A child's developmental level will have a great deal to do with the way he handles the strain of various experiences. It is important to remember that while adults suffer pain in a chronic manner, children suffer intermittently. They may be quite upset for awhile and then go out happily to play. That is normal. If the trauma is severe, such as the death of a parent or sibling, children will re-experience grief in a different way as they pass through each developmental stage.

Infants and Toddlers

Infants and toddlers have no cognitive understanding of death, illness, injury, divorce, and other life crises. They do respond, however, to the emotional well-being of their most

119

intimate caretakers. If the family is under stress, infants and toddlers will need more physical holding and touching than usual. Their lives also need to be kept routine as much as possible. If the primary care-taker can no longer assume that responsibility, it is better to transfer the care to one other person rather than sending the child from one care-taker to another. As a close friend or family member, offer to keep a child or toddler on an ongoing basis while the family goes through their crisis. If the child does not need to leave his home, go there often to give the child some special attention.

Pre-School To Age Seven

Children up to the age of six or seven think of life very concretely. Death, illness, and injury are best explained to them in honest physical terms. If someone has died, it should be explained in terms of the loved one no longer being able to breathe, eat, drink or feel. Children this age have no concept of death as eternal. Following is an example of the confusion a child this age can feel.

> When the hospital called to tell us the baby had died, I thought it was just for that day, so I went to bed and went to sleep. But the next morning, I heard them talking downstairs. The baby had still died, even though the hospital didn't call to tell us that day. I guessed it was going to take a few days, so we had a funeral. There was so much crying and standing around. When it was over, the baby had still died. When we got home, the refrigerator was broken. We got it fixed, but the baby had still died. Every morning, I kept asking if the baby had still died, and the answer was always 'yes.'

Children this age are more likely to act out their feelings in play than talk freely about them. They can act out their anger by hitting their toys, causing toy cars to collide, and building things and then smashing them. They may try to come to grips with death by burying themselves in a sandpile. Adult care-takers should be attentive to their play, ready to talk if the play leads into discussion of what's on their mind. Questions should be answered honestly. Children this age engage in much magical thinking and may conclude that something they did brought on the tragedy. Honest explanations will help them rid themselves of guilt. Because children this age may withdraw from their parents experiencing pain, you, as a close friend or relative, can provide an invaluable service to the entire family by taking the child on outings or into your home where free play is encouraged. The child may also talk more freely to you about his own feelings than he could to those in his own household.

Ages Seven to Eleven

Between the ages of seven and eleven, most children develop the capacity for understanding physical tragedies, such as death, injury, and illness, much as adults do. The more subtle components of divorce, separations, changes in status or income, are more difficult. You can be almost sure that children in this age range will find a way to blame themselves for what has happened. They will need ongoing discussion and explanations in an honest manner to help them evaluate the situation realistically.

Children of this age see death as all-powerful, something that can come to get them. This is evidenced by children's fascination with the power of evil forces at Halloween and in movies.

Children in this age range also have the capacity for empathy. They are able to focus beyond their feelings to the stresses of others. Many children attempt to be the "parent" for their grieving parents. This is a burden they should not have to carry. Parents going through divorces or separations must be especially cautious of drawing their child into a

121

vicious triangle which will leave him confused, angry, and depressed. As a close friend or relative, you may be in a unique position to invite the child to lunch on a regular basis and draw out feelings and fears. Because parents may be too focused on their own pain to be able to accommodate the child's pain, your friendship and support of the child can be very important.

Adolescents

Adolescents frequently react to pain and stress in the family by acting out or withdrawing. They still feel the frightening and vulnerable emotions of childhood, but they are afraid to let others see them cry. They may become upset because they don't want to be viewed as child-like. The insecurity of moving from childhood to adulthood, causes many adolescents to be shaky and self-centered. They find it difficult to think of anyone else's pain other than their own.

> The rest of the family went to the funeral home. My friends and I went out and shot baskets all afternoon. I didn't want to stand around and be sad all day.
>
> Teenager

Because of their normal psychological need to begin breaking away from their parents, adolescents have great difficulty focusing on pain within the family. While they need their family, they are trying hard to escape it. They are usually open to the friendship of other adults. They commonly refer to another adult as their "other mom" or "other dad." It is challenging and rewarding to provide this role for troubled adolescents. Offer the invitation. As an ally, you can provide stability and understanding they may never be able to find at home during those troubled times.

CHAPTER FIFTEEN

PLANNING AND ATTENDING FUNERALS

Those who have never experienced the death of a loved one may think of caskets, embalmed bodies, and funerals as frightening, foreign, and unnecessary. However, when someone dearly loved dies, they will probably long to express their pain in some acceptable way. They will want to cry. They will probably want to look at their loved one's body, even touch it, one last time. They will want all the world to know about the unique gifts their loved one gave to the world. And they will want those who love them to be near.

It is out of these longings that the tradition of funerals emerged. "Holding up well" through a ritualistic funeral is an inappropriate goal. Trying to force expression of grief in a particular way is an equally inappropriate goal. Providing a setting for letting go emotionally, loving and being loved by those who share the sorrow, and celebrating the uniqueness of the deceased loved one's life are far more meaningful goals. The funeral becomes a way of saying, "Stop and listen a minute, busy world! Listen to how much we loved this person who has died."

Funerals

If you are an acquaintance or a distant relative, attend the funeral, even if you do nothing else. Later, write a personal note of remembrance.

If you are a close friend or relative, you can be helpful in several other ways. Visit the home immediately after the death to share your grief with the family and assist with practical matters such as cleaning the house, doing the laundry, and food preparation. Provide items others won't think of: paper plates and cups, ice, a large coffee maker. Offer to make calls to relatives. Ask if you might be the official greeter for family members who prefer not to meet everyone who comes to their home. Take phone calls and record messages.

All those most intimately involved in the life of the deceased have a right to participate in the planning and orchestration of the funeral. Most funeral directors and clergy are willing to accommodate the desires of the family and close friends. These may encompass a simple, quiet graveside memorial consisting of only a few words, a formal, lengthy worship service held in a church, or a service in a school auditorium with many friends coming forward to remember the loved one in his or her own special way.

Suggest that family and close friends sit down together, even before clergy is called, to decide the tone of the funeral and who should be actively involved. Some families will not choose to involve themselves in much of the planning, leaving it entirely up to the funeral director and the clergy. That is totally acceptable. On the other hand, many families are not aware that they may have a choice in what happens at the funeral, and once informed will want to be involved in the planning.

If the family and close friends choose to plan the funeral, encourage all to share their ideas, including the children. If any of the children have never attended a funeral, this is a good time to explain their purpose.

Encourage them to express their ideas. As they help plan and participate, they will feel a part of the family and share their grieving. Discuss how the funeral can be personalized so that the life of the deceased is uniquely celebrated. Discuss how persons who wish to share in the event can do so. As a close friend or relative, do particular poems, songs, or Scriptures come to mind that you would like shared at the funeral? If so, say so. Perhaps you would like to prepare a poem or remembrance to be read.

Recently, a college professor was asked, "What helped the most when your wife died?" Without batting an eye, he responded, "The meaningfulness of the memorial service." He and his children decided that her body would be buried in a simple graveside service for family and a few close friends. After that, a loosely structured memorial service was held in one of the small auditoriums at the university. The service consisted almost entirely of friends and colleagues coming forward to tell what her life had meant to them. It was a celebration of her life. It validated her life and enabled all those who participated to focus on the beauty of who she was. They left more grateful for a life that had been lived and shared rather than being devastated by her loss.

The following remembrance was prepared by the seven grandchildren of a grandmother who died. The time spent in remembering the special things they loved most about their grandmother helped them to grieve as well as to capture her essence. All the grandchildren came forward at an appointed time during the funeral and stood together as the eldest grandson read the memorial.

A WOMAN OF GENTLE SPIRIT

We give thanks to God
    and celebrate the life
        of a dear Grandma
Who took the simplest of pleasures,
    Added her gentle and patient spirit,
        a dose of laughter,
And thereby, became a treasure to each of us.

A cherry pie baked as a special expression of love,
    Lemonade made with real lemons,
        After-school snacks
            lovingly prepared every afternoon
                Special treats enjoyed together at Pizza Hut,
                or Dairy Queen, or A & W.

"Oh my stars!, or "Land sakes," she would respond
    to the surprises of
        the Ringling Brothers Circus,
          a rodeo,
             a good hand of cards,
               or a funny joke.

How she savored and shared her joy
    over something as simple
        as a painting of the ocean and seagulls.

She cared "for the least of these"--
    A little dog named "Zippy," which she treated as a child,
        Any cat needing an extra patting,
           The child who wanted a bandaid
              whether needed or not,
                A lone petunia that might survive
                  with some TLC.

How carefully and lovingly she gave us gifts,
    Managing so carefully to be sure each one
        got an equally-priced Christmas present,
            Looking at every coloring book on the counter
            to choose the very best one.

A recent shopping spree with Allison,
    which resulted in a white fluffy teddy bear
        for Christmas...for Grandma--
            because Allison sensed how much she liked it!

And she listened...and listened, and listened,
    A confidante to each of us,
        Eager to sit down and hear us out,
            Offer a few words of wise insight,
            But never to tell us what to do.

We shall miss you.
    But we love you,
        We honor you,
            We celebrate you,
            And most of all, we thank you.

For by your gentle spirit, we have been blessed.

By Allana, Andrea, Allison, Chris, Lisa, Philip, and Robyn

    A copy of the poem and the white fluffy teddy bear were placed in their grandmother's casket before it was closed.

Funerals

When our daughter was killed, our family decided we wanted her buried on our family farm. We had recently moved into a new home several feet away from our old house which had burned, and the space which had been her old bedroom was now vacant. That's where we buried her. We keep yellow flowers on her grave (her favorite color) year round.

Mother

Sometimes I need to tell someone about the special funeral and about the things we put in his coffin. It's important to me, but some people think it's ghoulish and don't want me to talk about it.

Teenage son speaking of
his father's funeral

CHAPTER SIXTEEN

COPING WITH THE HOLIDAYS

It is easy to forget those who are in pain during the holidays. The reason is simple. As we enjoy Thanksgiving, Christmas, Mother's Day, and Father's Day with those we love, we don't want those times "spoiled" with thoughts or activities that remind us of the pain of others. While understandable, the friend or relative who wishes to be truly helpful will remember those who are hurting in some special way during the holidays.

A handwritten note, a single flower, or a book make wonderful statements of caring. Especially remember the birthday and death date of those now deceased. Remember wedding anniversaries of widows and widowers. Families of the deceased often say that these days are the loneliest because they sense that no one else remembers. While you may think it morbid to call attention to the death date or fear that it will resurrect the pain, that is rarely, if ever, true. The death date, particularly if the loved one was suddenly killed, is imprinted indelibly in their minds. If you were to ask these people to tell you what happened, nearly all would begin telling the story by stating the date. It will matter significantly to them to know that you, too, remembered.

As a close friend or relative, one of the most helpful things you can do is help the hurting person plan how they will spend the forthcoming holiday. For them to sit idly by and let the dreaded day "happen" will likely prove disastrous. Instead, help them plan, almost on an hourly basis, what they can do to get through the holiday as painlessly as possible. You can't insist on an activity, but you can offer options.

Openly Discuss Traditions And How To Handle Them.

If a family member is now absent and Christmas is coming, talk about whether it might be easier to change the tradition. Discuss what is to be done with the Christmas stocking and tree ornaments made or purchased by that person and about whether or not to put up a tree this year. As Father's Day approaches, and a special Father's Day cookout has always been held at one place, consider changing the place or the menu. If Valentine's Day is approaching and a love relationship has ended, help the sorrowing person to think of other persons whom they love, even if not romantically, and do something special for or with them. Trying to avoid holidays is usually futile because the rest of society is celebrating and it is impossible to escape. Taking control of the holiday is the better option.

Create a Special Tribute For The Day.

Since the grieving often lament that a "conspiracy of silence" seems to exist within the family at holiday time, help them find a special way to acknowledge the memory of their loved one. One family in which a child was killed, gets together first thing on Christmas morning, places flowers on their loved one's grave and says through their own meditations, "Merry Christmas. We haven't forgotten you today." They then go home to spend the rest of the day doing the traditional things, feeling that she has been remembered.

Offer Practical Help.

Take in food. Offer to help with Christmas shopping and wrapping. Help clean the home if relatives are coming. Mow the grass. Wash the car. If the person is spending the day alone, invite him or her to your home or visit them for an hour or two. If the person observes religious rituals, offer to drive or accompany them.

Help Discover A Creative Outlet.

Suggest that a poem be read and shared or a flower arrangement be sent to a church, nursing home, or hospital in memory of the deceased loved one. One mother, who always baked gingerbread houses at Christmas time for her children, was able to resume the tradition a few years after her children were killed and gave them away to others who would enjoy them. Another mother whose teenage daughter had been killed by a drunk driver invited a large group of her daughter's friends to meet the night before New Year's Eve. They lighted candles in her memory, and the mom urged them to not drink and drive on New Year's Eve.

Suggest Reaching Out To A Fellow Sufferer.

As has been mentioned previously, the best way to overcome emotional pain is to fully experience it, and then reach out to help someone else in similar pain. The most creative way your hurting friend might help himself or herself, is to spend the holiday time reaching out to others. The lonely, rejected lover or spouse might extend an invitation to another lonely person to spend the day together doing something that both would enjoy. He or she might purchase two tickets to a play or concert and invite another to come along. The injured person might make a special phone call to someone else injured or, if they are able, visit others more seriously injured in the hospital.

Holidays

More important than what you actually do is the fact that you remember and know that holidays will be tough for the person in pain. Your friend's loneliness will be exaggerated. As a caring friend or relative, your presence, acknowledgement of the pain, and willingness to help with creative planning about how to spend the day will be treasures not soon, if ever, forgotten.

CHAPTER SEVENTEEN

UNDERSTANDING SPIRITUAL
AND MYSTICAL EXPERIENCES

Faith Concerns

> When my daughter was killed at age twenty-four, I felt anguish--like I wanted to pull my hair out. At times my body-wrenching sobs would abate when I cried out, "God help me." I believe He did for a moment. My rapid breathing would slow down and a feeling of calm would wash over me. But it didn't last long.
>
> Mother whose daughter was
> brutally murdered

When death, physical illness or injury, or emotional pain intrudes into one's life, most people tend to cry out to God, perhaps for the first time in their lives. For many, it is a longing to make sense of something senseless. For others, it is a cry for release from pain.

Spiritual Experiences

Your friend or relative, deeply in distress, may lament, "How can I believe in a God who would let this happen?" If your faith is important to you, and especially if you feel that most of your own theological questions have been answered, you may feel that you need to proclaim "an answer."

People in pain usually find theological "answers" less than satisfactory. Phrases like "It was God's will" or "All things have a purpose" leave them angry and wondering what they have done to deserve it, if it was God's will. Such phrases frequently add torment to torment.

Some will choose to conclude on their own that it was God's will and try to find a reason for it. It is their responsibility to find a framework of meaning for their loss, and this may be the way they do it. However, it is not wise to impose such a theology on them, since the risk of inflicting additional anguish is great.

The more honest and acceptable response is simply, "There are so many things in life that can't be explained and this is one of them." Many people who have wrestled with their faith after a tragedy conclude that most of the suffering in the world results from the fact that human beings have free wills, and the choices they sometimes make result in pain and suffering. They feel that while God may seem to be present and stand with them in their suffering, He rarely lifts them from it or enables them to totally escape it. They find comfort in the belief that God's heart is broken, too, by their pain.

> After the children were killed, a lot of people talked about God as if He had done it. However, one dear friend simply held me and said, "I'll bet God is crying today, too." That was wonderfully helpful.
>
> Mother whose son and his fiancee were killed in a vehicular crash

If you have thought through a theology of suffering of your own, it is acceptable for you to share it. But, offer it only as one alternative for belief. Personal faith issues are among the most difficult to resolve. Honestly faithful persons will not take them lightly. They do not want someone else's theology pushed down their throat, but they can be receptive if it is offered as a suggestion.

The Bible, as well as the Scriptures of other faiths, contain many stories about the anger, frustration, and grieving not only of human beings, but of God Himself. Your friend or relative may find it meaningful to know that these "dark" emotions are acceptable.

Eli Wiesel, Nobel Peace Prize winning Jewish theologian, relates an old Jewish legend built around the destruction of Jerusalem. In the story, God entered the burning sanctuary of the Temple, and, seeing the flames, began to weep. Jeremiah was standing by. God summoned the prophet to go and wake up the Fathers of the people. He said, "Wake up Abraham and Isaac and Jacob. And Moses, wake him too. Tell them I wish to see them. I need them because they know how to weep."

Most people who take their faith seriously struggle with the issue of forgiveness if their suffering results from someone else's bad choice. The criminal justice system process prevents criminal offenders, even if sorry for their actions, from expressing it. Defense attorneys counsel the offender to stay away from the victim and the victim's family for fear that any words uttered will be taken as a legal admission of guilt. However, many of the victims who are sought out by the offender find that the expression of remorse seldom relieves pain. The pain results more from the loss than the commission of the crime.

Spiritual Experiences

The mother of a woman who had been killed by a hit-and-run drunk driver longed for the driver to say he was sorry. At the end of his trial he rose and said:

'I'd like to apologize to the relatives and family. This is a sickening crime, and I feel sick. I don't expect you to forgive me or like me for any reason, but, I want you to know I...I wish this had not happened.'

After the trial was dismissed the mother began to sob and said, "I always wanted him to say he was sorry, and now he does...and...she's still gone."

You might suggest, if the issue is forgiveness, that genuine forgiveness of someone who has deeply hurt another is a very difficult task. Trying to forgive some one who is not remorseful can feel wrong. It may take time to do that. It might be helpful to suggest that forgiving does not mean forgetting. It will be impossible to forget what has happened, and it should not be expected.

Mystical Experiences

Persons deeply in distress, whether grieving the loss of a loved one or in personal physical pain, often report mystical experiences. People who have been clinically dead but returned to life report amazingly similar experiences of being "out of their bodies," traveling through a tunnel with a bright and warm light at the end, seeing loved ones just ahead to greet them, and very often seeing the primary focus of their religion, such as Jesus or Buddha.

I feel my work with children who are dying has enriched my life. Their simple faith has convinced me there is a Heaven. It's not unusual for children to know the day they are dying and for them to see visions of angels and Jesus. It's utterly amazing to see them interact with someone we're unable to see. Their eyes are so bright and their smiles are so big, you know it's not a hallucination.

A Registered Nurse

Those mourning the death of a loved one sometimes report that they awoke in the night, sat up in bed, and "saw" their loved one, as if they had come back to assure them that all was well. Some have reported hearing the voice of their loved one give them a message in the middle of the day when their minds were far from the memory of that person. Others report the sudden blooming of a tree or flower that hadn't bloomed for years within a few days of a loved one's death.

While these reports may seem "spooky," or like figments of the imagination so many of them are now being reported that it is difficult to deny their reality. Most people who have mystical experiences, while unable to prove that they really happened, are so convinced of their reality that no amount of doubtful coercion can convince them otherwise. If they are taken simply for what they appear to be, a caring friend or relative has no need to discredit them.

On the other hand, if the mystical experience seems to keep the person linked in an unhealthy way to the experience and diminishes their quality of life, intervention may become necessary. For example, if a mother believes that the spirit of her deceased daughter returned to visit her once when she was in the daughter's room and that revelation is now more important to her than anything else in her life, she may be in danger. She is in even more danger if she decides to keep the room exactly as it is and does not allow anyone to enter it, converting it into a shrine. In that event, a single isolated mystical experience has now been generalized to every area of her life.

If your friend or family member has had a mystical experience which seems to be positive and which has not caused a breakdown in other areas of his or her life, you have no reason to try to discredit it. Some have pointed out that birth and death are so mystical in and of themselves, that other mysterious circumstances should not come as a shock to us.

If troubling theological concerns or mystical experiences which have a negative, all-encompassing effect are bothering your friend or family member, help him or her locate a licensed pastoral counselor or minister who has experience counseling those deeply in pain. Word of mouth is usually the best referral source, so search for other faithful persons who can recommend someone who has helped them. Some books on this topic are listed in the resource section of this book. They could make useful gifts for your loved one.

CHAPTER EIGHTEEN

SUGGESTING COUNSELING

You may think that counseling will help your friend or relative to better cope. You face several dilemmas. You may not be certain that counseling is actually needed, know of any good counselors, or know how to suggest counseling without causing offense.

Knowing whether or not counseling is needed is difficult because normal grieving symptoms frequently parallel those of classic depression. While good counseling can benefit anyone, the decision can only be made by the person hurting. The one exception to that is suicide or homicide. If you sense that your friend or family member is suicidal or homicidal, you must not expect them to seek counseling on their own. You should consider taking charge, even at the risk of betraying confidentiality or damaging your relationship. The place for a suicidal person is in a suicide prevention center or hospital emergency room. Homicidal people need to be hospitalized and evaluated. Chapter Nineteen, **Preventing Suicide**, can help you evaluate the potential for suicide.

Since all losses involve grieving, grieving symptoms are normal, not abnormal. As noted previously, injured and ill people grieve the loss of body function and physical appearance, loss of the joy of work satisfaction, and the loss of dreams which now must go unfulfilled. Persons going through divorce or separation grieve not only the loss of the person but also the loss of their own image as someone who is loved. They grieve the loss of companionship and relationship, and the loss of their role as a lover. Therefore, they suffer many of the same symptoms as those grieving a death: crying, withdrawal, fatigue, anger, eating and sleeping problems, loss of sexual drive, difficulty concentrating, confusion, and lack of direction. Any one of these symptoms do not necessarily mean that counseling is needed. As a caring friend or family member, you would be wise to evaluate the number, intensity, and duration of the symptoms.

Several of the symptoms together can render the person in need of medical care or evaluation for short term, anti-depressant medication. Failure to eat and sleep over an extended period of time can affect the body's immune system drastically and make people susceptible to a number of illnesses. Generally, the more symptoms that exist, the greater the need for help.

Any one of the symptoms intensely experienced can also mean trouble. Extreme confusion or refusal to eat are warning signs. Increased use of alcohol or other drugs to escape the emotional pain is a clear warning signal. Hallucinations (seeing or hearing things which aren't there) or delusions (distorted thinking based on non-reality) after a few weeks are also clear calls for help. These may be considered normal at first, and can even be medication-induced, but are clearly problematic if they continue.

Duration of symptoms is the most difficult evaluation tool because it may vary extensively. Most people begin to feel a little better after a few weeks or months. However, following sudden, violent deaths, such as vehicular crashes or murders, especially if the loved one was a child, symptoms can exist for years.

As you try to assess the emotional condition of your friend or relative, look for the following:

o   Do you see change, even though minor, in your friend or relative's grieving pattern? Is it better now than it was a month ago, a week ago? Do you see a shift, even though gradual, from focus on the loss to focus on life as it may exist now and in the future?

o   Can you see that a distinction is being made between sorrow over what has been lost and chronic, ongoing depression? What has happened will never be forgotten, but in time, it should be only a part of the life experience, not all of it.

o   Do grief spasms occur from time to time, becoming less intense, shorter in duration, and less frequent as time goes on?

If you can answer "yes" to these questions, your friend or family member may not <u>need</u> counseling. However, they may enjoy some benefits of counseling if they decide to go. They can find relief in being able to talk honestly about their feelings with someone who can be objective and provide confidentiality. They may find it a comfort to learn that they are not "crazy" and that most people experiencing similar losses feel much the same as they do. Having one's experience normalized is comforting and reassuring.

Finding an appropriate counselor is not an easy task. As you turn to the yellow pages of your phone book and look under the headings "counseling, mental health", "counseling, religious," "mental health," "psychiatrists," "psychologists," "psychotherapists," and "social workers," you may feel frustrated with all the titles and specializations. Just as there are a myriad of specializations within physical medicine, there are different areas of interest within the field of counseling.

Counseling

Word-of-mouth from a person who has experienced a similar loss and was satisfied with their counseling or direct referral from a specialist is a better resource for choosing a counselor than the phone book. Most physicians who deal with illness and injury can suggest counselors who specialize in helping people cope with those particular issues. Hospital social workers, hospice programs, and chaplains can usually give names of good grief counselors. Rape crisis centers and domestic violence programs often screen community counselors and know who can work best with victims of those crimes. Mental Health Associations can usually suggest good counselors for those experiencing divorces or loss of love relationships.

Support Groups, such as Mothers Against Drunk Driving, Compassionate Friends, or Parents of Murdered Children, frequently have referral lists of counselors who have been helpful to their members. Victim/Witness programs located in police departments or prosecutors' offices can make good counseling referrals for those who have been criminally violated. In many states, these offices provide application forms for reimbursement of counseling fees for crime victims through State Victim Compensation programs. If criminal or civil law suits are filed against offenders, it is also possible to require the offender to pay for the victim's counseling through restitution in a criminal case or as a condition of a civil settlement. Counselors working with clients involved in any kind of criminal or civil litigation owe it to their clients to fully understand those systems and the relative laws in their state.

After you have determined that counseling would be beneficial, and you have the names of one or two counselors you think would be appropriate, broaching the subject is your next task. Honesty is always the best approach. If they don't bring up the subject, you might say:

> 'It has been my experience that most people hurting as badly as you do benefit from counseling. I wish I could be all you need, but I'm frustrated as a friend. As much as I love you, I'm not able to give you the help you need and deserve. (Explain your search.) I have come up with a couple of names of therapists who sound good. I'll leave the names and numbers here for you, if you decide to go.'

Most people know when they need counseling. They know because they feel "stuck," their symptoms are not improving, and the pain is too difficult to bear. But others, even though they may not actually "need" counseling, will appreciate your concern and the work you have put into enabling them to feel better. Remember, though, that the decision is theirs, and they have the right to make it in their own due time. Do not be disappointed if your friend or family member does not respond immediately. You have done your part, and the next move is theirs.

CHAPTER NINETEEN

PREVENTING SUICIDE

Someone you love may be so depressed, confused, or frustrated that you fear that suicide is being considered. If so, you may not only prove yourself to be a supportive friend by attempting to rescue him or her from this devastating act, but you may actually save a life.

> Two things enabled me to decide not to commit suicide after all. One was thinking about how much it would hurt my family, and the other was my belief that I would not join my children in heaven if I did it.
>
> Woman whose four children
> were murdered

Here are a few things you should know about suicide. Most people who attempt suicide have talked about it with one or more persons. Warnings and clues are usually given. Being attentive to those clues and talking about the possibility and results of a suicide do not make the person commit suicide. In fact, talking about the idea of suicide and its aftermath is usually the very thing that helps one decide not to do it.

Very few people who attempt suicide truly want to die. Most are ambivalent. They want to live but consider suicide because they fear that they can't find a way to escape the pain they face.

On the other hand, be especially cautious if the person who has been suicidal suddenly seems to feel better and have a more positive outlook on life. It may mean that the suicide plan has been completed and a suicidal decision made. In this case stopping the suicide can be difficult, so ask clearly if they are still planning suicide. If you sense that they are, don't leave their side until you can get help.

Evaluating the Potential for Suicide

Most, but not all, suicidal persons are depressed. Consider these questions: Has your friend experienced a depressing loss such as a love relationship, a job, or his own physical ability? Has there been a death of someone close to him or her? Has there been a loss of dreams? Do you see signs of depression, such as lack of interest in food, friends, work, activities? Is the person now sloppy in appearance? Does he or she experience insomnia or seem to be sleeping all the time? Has he withdrawn from previously meaningful relationships?

Persons who have previously attempted suicide are at greater risk of attempting it again. So are those whose relative, friend, or even acquaintance has recently committed suicide. It makes suicide a more viable option. If either of these is the case, you need to be doubly cautious.

Recall if your friend or relative has verbalized statements of personal hopelessness such as:

"I see no reason to go on living."

"I don't think I will ever feel better."

"Nothing could make it any better for me."

"I just want it to be over."

"It will be better for you if I'm gone."

Has your friend or relative recently given away valuable possessions such as cars, jewelry, money, items of personal significance? Has there been an attempt to "put things in order" by updating wills or changing life insurance policies?

It is true that many depressed and sorrowing people truly wish to die to escape the emotional pain. People experiencing chronic physical pain also often wish to die to escape it. However, most of them do not commit suicide. The strong wish to die usually lasts only a few hours at a time, or, at worst, a few days. They either "wait it out," hanging on to the thread of hope that it will get better, or find they don't have the skill, determination, or willingness to kill themselves.

If someone is down and says 'I just want to die,' don't everyone run to the gun cabinet or medicine cabinet to do a quick count. Wanting to die so you can be with your loved one and contemplating suicide are definitely not the same. I've prayed to God to let me die so I could be with her again, but then asked His forgiveness for daring to ask such a thing. Talking about these feelings always helps.

Husband whose wife had been killed

Begin by stating your concern clearly: "You seem to be in a lot of pain. Is it so bad that you've thought about suicide?" or "When was the last time you thought about suicide?" or "How often do you think about suicide?"

If your friend or relative has seriously considered suicide, or if he or she is considering it now, ask if they have a suicidal plan. Talking about it will not cause them to carry out the plan. Those who are ambivalent will probably tell you about their plan. More likely, talking about it will remove some of the mysticism from it. It helps the person better understand everything that can happen during and after a completed suicide.

If there is a plan, your next step is to determine if the weapon or other lethal means is actually available. Usually, the more complete and specific the suicide plan, especially if the means are available, the higher the risk of suicide.

If the answers to these questions leave you concerned, your next goal is to create the idea in your friend's mind that there are other ways to relieve some of the pain. Look your friend in the eye, touch him or her, and say: "Listen to me. I love you, and I don't want you to do that. I think there are some other alternatives. Is there any reason you couldn't wait to explore some other possibilities?"

Preventing Suicide

All suicide threats should be taken seriously, especially those including a clear, detailed plan. Following are suggestions for keeping a person alive until you can arrange for professional help:

o **Don't panic.**

o **Listen** to why he or she wants to die without making judgments or trying to talk him or her out of it.

o **Don't try to minimize it.** The person will only feel less understood. Avoid phrases such as, "It's really not as bad as you think it is."

o **Express personal care** for the person. Talk about what he or she means to you and how you would feel if the suicidal decision were made. Think of family and friends you believe the suicidal person cares about. Ask how these individuals would respond to the suicide. If pictures of these persons are available, refer to them.

o **Be aware** that some people who suicide do so to hurt someone else. In that case <u>don't</u> focus on how that person will respond.

o **Take charge** if you have the slightest hint that suicide might be imminent. This is not a time for reflective listening or democratic problem solving. Assure your friend or relative that while their pain is intense, suicidal urges are temporary and that help is available to relieve the pain. Get the suicidal person to the hospital.

o **Understand that saving a life supersedes confidentiality and friendship.** If the person is truly suicidal, he or she will later be grateful to you for your intervention. If not, he or she may be angry at your intrusiveness at first, but will probably be grateful later that you cared enough to intervene.

PART V

CONCLUSION

CHAPTER TWENTY

TIME AND RECOVERY

The significance of time can't be overlooked. Recovery can't be pushed or coerced. No matter how skilled you have become in supporting your friend or family member, time is an essential component in healing.

Some people fully recover from the losses they experience. Those who lose something or someone very precious to them seldom fully recover. They don't get over it--they just get used to it.

Most people are surprised at how long it takes to get better after one has experienced a traumatic loss.

My daughter still has nightmares. She's afraid to even take out the garbage. My assault made her terrified of boys--even her own cousins. She's only nine years old.

Victim of sexual assault

It's been two years since my daughter was killed. I am still depressed. I can't hold down an eight-hour job.

> Mother whose daughter was
> killed in a vehicular crash

Our society expects people to recover from losses very quickly. People tire of listening and supporting. Their abandonment of those the victim counted on hurts deeply.

I needed to talk about the accident, but when I started telling my closest friend about it the second time, she got angry and told me I was treating her as if I thought she were stupid because I had already told her once. She said she would get back in touch with me when I was "healthy."

> Seriously injured vehicular
> crash victim

It's been years and it still hurts every time I think about her.

> Man whose lover left him

After eighteen months in psychotherapy, I have learned to live with the anger, frustrations, rage, and guilt I feel in trying to cope with my injuries.

> Vehicular crash victim

Efforts to "hurry up" one's healing will be resented. Therefore, it is best to avoid such comments as:

"Aren't you over that yet?"

"You've got to get on with your life."

"You need to be strong for _____'s sake."

"You shouldn't still be feeling this way."

Instead, consider the following:

"In time, you will feel better than you do now. But for now, try to be patient with yourself. You've been through a lot."

"Try not to judge yourself by others' expectations of you. Only you know what is best for you."

"Spasms of grief are very normal and will probably continue periodically for a long time. That doesn't mean that you're going crazy or you're not making progress."

Some think that keeping very busy as a means of avoiding the pain will help, but over-activity should be discouraged. It is easy to jump into a new relationship too soon, make decisions about property and possessions before one can think clearly, and join activist groups too quickly, simply as a means of occupying time. A good rule of thumb is to make no major decisions for at least a year after a significant life change.

Becoming re-established in one's social world after a loss is not easy. Because of the experience, your friend or family member is not the same person, so attempts to return to the status quo are complicated and take time.

A formerly married person may feel uncomfortable in his or her old social group where everyone else is married. Unfortunately, others in the group may even be threatened or jealous if they fear that the newly-separated person is a potential candidate for a new type of relationship with a group member of the opposite sex.

The ill or injured person may be perceived as a handicap to the activity of the old social group. One woman who suffered multiple injuries in a vehicular crash was told by one of her friends that she should now seek "her own kind" for friends.

If your friend or family member is disappointed by the lack of care and attention offered by their old social group, he or she may no longer wish to spend time with them. That is a painful decision.

As a supportive helper, you can assist your friend or family member in evaluating their return to society. Be aware that your time-frame may not be the same as theirs, but honor it.

If it is determined that the old social group is no longer acceptable, seek a new one. That takes effort. Various groups of persons experiencing similar losses are a potential source of new friends. Organizations listed in the back of this book can provide colleagues who understand the pain. They have had similar experiences. They can become closer than family or friends who can't comprehend it.

I found that the best way to lose my own self-pity was to reach out to others going through the same thing. It helped them, but it also helped me.

Woman who became active in
Mothers Against Drunk Driving
after her child was killed

On the other hand, it is not wise to limit one's social world to fellow sufferers. An unrealistic world-view can develop. Churches, civic organizations, college classes, and other groups which contain all kinds of people can offer opportunities for new friendships.

Remember that your friend or family member, more than you, knows when social re-involvement feels right. It may take longer than you think. Trust their judgment.

Be cautious about prematurely putting your friend or family member in a setting that will emphasize the loss. For example, if they have lost a spouse or lover, don't put them in the company of the opposite sex until <u>they</u> indicate a readiness. Parents who have lost a child find it very difficult to be in the presence of other children the same age. Handicapped people sometimes resent being introduced to other handicapped people and being expected to like them, just because they, too, are handicapped.

"Two no's mean no!" is a good rule to follow. Invite your friend or family member to go with you to some outing or event. If the answer is "no" respect it. It will be fine, however, to ask again in a day or two. Perhaps by then, they will change their mind. If the answer is still "no," trust that they are simply not ready and drop it.

I appreciated being asked to go places, but I also appreciated it when my friends accepted my refusal. In time, I was ready to say 'yes.'

Widow whose husband died

Time, patience, genuine caring, and skills in knowing what to say and do are the winning combination for enabling healing. These are better than just saying "I'm sorry."

Caring in this way can be sacrificial and sometimes painful. But your friend or loved one in pain is worth it. Your reward will be great if you are willing to risk offering yourself beyond a simple expression of sympathy.

APPENDIX

SAMPLE NOTES

Death Following Illness

Dear _____,

I have thought of you so often during _____'s illness and wished I could ease your burden. I'm sure your heart must have broken time and time again to watch the suffering of someone you loved so much.

My thoughts are now on _____ and the special things he/she brought to my life. I remember when . . . .

I am sorry for all he/she endured, and I am also glad he/she was born and lived. I will keep you in my prayers.

Fondly,

Sudden Death

Dear_____,

I couldn't believe it when I learned of _____'s death. I can't imagine how you endured the shock of it all. It may still seem like a terrible nightmare to you.

While still reeling in the news of his/her death, I am also recalling what a very special person he/she was. I remember . . . .

Please take care of yourself, _____. Grieving a sudden death is so hard when you long to have been able to say "Good-bye" and "I love you" but didn't have the opportunity. Try to spend as much time as you can with the people you love the most. Sharing grief with dear family and friends really helps, even though it hurts. You will be in my thoughts and prayers.

Most sincerely,

Suicide

Dear _____,

I was so saddened to hear of_____'s death. I imagine you are trying to put the pieces together, although it is impossible to understand all the whys and wherefores.

I want you to know what I think of when I think of ____.
He/she . . . .

And now my thoughts turn to you and what you must be going through. I can't begin to understand how difficult this must be, but I also know that no matter what you might have done or not done, the decision was made by _____. I'm sure he/she felt it was the best one to make.

Please be gentle with yourself during the next weeks and months. I will be thinking of you.

Sincerely,

Terminal Illness

Dear _____,

I was thinking about you today and decided to write a note to tell you so! I'd love to spend some time with you but realize you may not be up to it.

That doesn't stop me, though, from thinking about the time we . . . .

I guess neither of us knows just what the future holds. I long for your recovery, and at the same time understand that it may or may not come. While saddened by your illness, I so celebrate your life! In case you don't realize the gift your life is to me, I want to say now . . . .

With much respect,

Serious Injury

Dear _____,

I was thinking about you today and trying to imagine how painful and frustrating it must be to try to overcome an injury like yours. I'm sure I can't begin to understand.

You may not feel strong, but I wish you the courage to keep trying to get better, even if it's just a little each day. I am so sorry about what happened to you but I'm glad you're alive! Your specialness to me wasn't touched by your injury.

Hang in there!

Loved Ones of the Ill or Injured

Dear _____,

You were on my mind today, so I decided to drop you a note to wish you some peace and strength as you face _____'s pain. Watching someone you love suffer must feel unbearable sometimes.

I remember the time you meant so much to me when _____ _____. I know you are even more special to _____ although his/her pain and frustration probably get taken out on you sometimes.

You are all in my thoughts and prayers,

Loss of a Love/Divorce

Dear _____,

I was thinking about you today and trying to imagine the hurt. I guess there are good and bad parts about the ending of any relationship and I don't pretend to understand all this means for you.

But I do hold you in my heart and in my mind, and wish you peace.

Your friend ,

Forced Retirement/Job Loss

Dear _____,

I heard about your retirement/job loss and want you to know I'm thinking about you. I guess there are always good parts and bad parts of change, and I don't pretend to know all this means for you.

At any rate, I value my relationship with you and look forward to its continuation, just as always. Who you are means a lot more to me than what you do!

Respectfully,

RECOMMENDED BOOKS

DEATH

For Adults

Brooks, Anne M., *The Grieving Time: A Year's Account of Recovery From Loss,* The Dial Press, Doubleday & Co., Inc., Garden City, NY (Once-a-month journal entries for a year following her husband's death from cancer.)

Donnelly, Katherine, *How to Recover From the Loss of a Sibling,* Dodd, Mead, & Co., 71 Fifth Ave., New York, NY 10003.

Donnelly, Katherine, *Recovering From the Loss of a Child,* Macmillan Publishing Company, Front and Brown Streets, Riverside, N.J. 08370.

Donnelly, Katherine, *Recovering From the Loss of a Parent,* Dodd, Mead, & Co., 71 Fifth Ave., New York, NY 10003.

Loewinsohn, Ruth J., *Survival Handbook for Widows,* Scott, Foresman, & Co., 1900 E. Lake Ave., Glenview, Ill 60025.

Schafer, Dan, and Lyons, Christine, *How Do We Tell the Children?* Newmarket Press, 3 East 48th St., New York, NY 10017. (Helps parents explain death to children at different age levels)

Schiff, Harriet S., *Living Through Mourning,* Viking Penguin, Inc. 40 West 23rd Street, New York, NY 10010.

Schiff, Harriet S., *The Bereaved Parent,* Penguin Books, 40 W. 23rd Street, New York, NY 10017.

For Small Children

Clardy, Andrea F., *Dusty Was My Friend,* Human Sciences Press, 72 Fifth Avenue, New York, NY 10011. (A school friend is killed in a vehicular crash)

Green, Phyllis, *A New Mother for Martha,* Human Sciences Press, 72 Fifth Avenue, New York, NY 10011. (Father remarries after the death of a child's mother)

Heegaard, Marge, *When Someone Very Special Dies,* Woodland Press, 99 Woodland Circle, Minneapolis, MN 55424.

Jukes, Mavis, *Blackberries in the Dark,* Dell Publishing, 1 Dag Hammarskjold Plaza, 245 E. 47th St., New York, NY 10017. (Death of a Grandfather)

Mellonie, Bryan and Ingpen, Robert, *Lifetimes,* Bantam Books, 666 Fifth Avenue, New York, NY 10103. (Beautiful picture book to be read to small children)

For Adolescents

Blume, Judy, *Tiger Eyes,* Dell Publishing, 1 Dag Hammarskjold Plaza, 245 E. 47th St., New York, NY 10017. (Father of an adolescent girl is killed)

Richter, Elizabeth, *Losing Someone You Love: When a Brother or Sister Dies,* G. P. Putnam's Sons, 51 Madison Avenue, New York, NY 10010. (Youth ages 10-21 write about the death of their sibling)

Rosen, Helen, *Unspoken Grief: Coping with Childhood Sibling Loss,* Lexington Books, Lexington, MA.

SUDDEN DEATH

Cato, Sid, *Healing Life's Great Hurts,* Chicago Review Press, 213 Institute Place, Chicago, IL 60610.

Lord, Janice Harris, *No Time For Goodbyes: Coping with Sorrow, Anger, and Injustice After a Tragic Death,* Pathfinder Publishing, 458 Dorothy Avenue, Ventura, CA 93003.

SUICIDE

Lukas, Christopher & Seiden, Henry, *Silent Grief: Living in the Wake of Suicide,* Macmillan, 866 Third Ave., New York, NY 10022.

Bolton, Iris, *My Son, My Son, . . . A Guide To Healing After a Suicide in the Family,* Bolton Press, 1325 Belmore Way, NE, Atlanta, GA 30338

DEATH AND FAITH

Granger, Westberg, *Good Grief,* Fortress Press, 2900 Queen Lane, Philadelphia, PA 19129.

Lewis, C.S., *A Grief Observed,* Seabury Press (Harper Religious Books), Keystone Industrial Park, Scranton, PA 18512.

Lindbergh, Ann, *Hour of Lead: Sharing Sorrow,* Redpath Press, 3137 Holmes Ave. South, Minneapolis, MN 55408.

Wolterstorff, N., *Lament for a Son,* Wm. B. Eerdmans Publishing Co., 255 Jefferson Ave. SE, Grand Rapids, MI 49503.

SERIOUS ILLNESS

Home Health Care Handbook: A Guide for the Family of the Homebound Patient, National Health Publishing Company, 99 Pointers Mill Road, Owings Mills, MD 21117.

Gordon, Jacqueline, *Give Me One Wish,* W.W. Norton & Co., 500 Fifth Ave., New York, NY 10010.

Wheeler, Eugenie G. & Dace-Lombard, Joyce, *Living Creatively With Chronic Illness: Transcending The Loss, Pain and Frustration,* Pathfinder Publishing, 458 Dorothy Ave., Ventura, CA 93003.

AIDS

Peabody, Barbara, *The Screaming Room,* Avon Publishing (A Division of United Methodist Publishing House), 201 Eighth Ave. S., Nashville, TN 37202.

Surviving and Thriving With AIDS, People With AIDS Coalition, 1012 14th St, NW, Suite 601, Washington, D.C.

Head Injury

Campbell, Kay and Miller, Constance, *From the Ashes: A Head Injury Self-Advocacy Guide,* Options Press, Box 1020- A195, Kirkland, WA 98033

Warrington, Janette, *The Humpty Dumpty Syndrome*, National Head Injury Foundation, 333 Turnpike Road, Southborough, MA 01772.

CRIME VICTIMIZATION

Austern, David, *The Crime Victim's Handbook,* Penguin Books.

Bard, Morton & Sangrey, Dawn, *The Crime Victim's Book,* Brunner/Mazel, Psychological Stress Series, 19 Union Square, New York, NY 10003. (Gives an excellent overview of victimization and the needs of various types of victims)

Komlos, Sharon, *Feel the Laughter,* Trillium Press, Inc. PO Box 209, Monroe, NY 10950. (Sharon was shot in the eyes, raped, and assaulted and survived with a healthy attitude even though blinded)

LeDray, Linda, *Recovering From Rape,* Holt, Rinehart, & Winston, Inc., 383 Madison Ave., New York, NY 10017.

164

Rouse, Linda, *You Are Not Alone: A Guide for Battered Women*, Learning Publications, PO Box 1326, Holmes Beach, FL 33509.

Saldana, Theresa, *Beyond Survival*, Bantam Books, 666 Fifth Avenue., New York, NY 10103. (Theresa is a stabbing victim. This is an excellent book for anyone suffering serious injury.)

Straus, M.A., Gelles, S.K. & Steinmetz, S.K., *Behind Closed Doors: Violence in the American Family*, Doubleday and Anchor Press.

LOSS OF A LOVE

Colgrove, Melba & Bloomfield, Harold, *How to Survive the Loss of a Love*, Bantam Books Inc., 666 Fifth Ave., New York, NY 10103.

Matteson, Judith, *Divorce: The Pain and the Healing*, Augsburg Publishing, 426 S. Fifth, Minneapolis, MN 55440.

Smith, Harold Ivan, *I Wish Someone Understood My Divorce*, Augsburg Publishing, 426 S. Fifth, Minneapolis, MN 55440.

Tomkins, Judy, *Coming Back: Recovering from the Breakup of a Marriage*, E.P. Dutton, 2 Park Ave., New York, NY 10016.

.

HELPFUL ORGANIZATIONS

AIDS

o   National Association of People With AIDS
1012 14th Street NW, Suite 601
Washington, D.C. (202-429-2856)

o   Federation of Parents and Friends of Lesbians and Gays
Box 24565
Los Angeles, CA 90024 (213) 472-8952)

Cancer

o   American Cancer Society
90 Park Avenue
New York, NY. 10016 (212-586-8700)

o   The Candlelighters Childhood Cancer Foundation   1901
Pennsylvania Avenue, NW, Suite 1001
Washington, D.C. 20006   (202-659-5136)

Crime Victims

o   National Organization for Victim Assistance (NOVA)
717 D Street NW
Washington, D.C. 20004 (202-393-NOVA)

o   National Victim Center
307 W. 7th St, Suite 1001
Fort Worth, TX 76102   (817-877-3355)

o   Victims for Victims
1800 S. Robertson Blvd., Bldg. 6, Suite 400
Los Angeles, CA 90035   (213-850-5001)

o   National Victim's Resource Center
P.O. Box 6000
Rockville, MD 20850
301-251-5525

Death of Child

o   Center for Sibling Loss
The Southern School
1456 West Montrose
Chicago, Ill., 60613   (312-769-0185)

o   Compassionate Friends
PO Box 3696
Oak Brook, IL 60522   (312-990-0010)

o   Share, St. John's Hospital
800 E. Carpenter Street
Springfield, IL 62769   (217-544-6464)

Domestic Violence

o   National Clearinghouse on Domestic Violence
P.O. Box 2309
Rockville, MD 20852

o   National Coalition Against Domestic Violence
P.O. Box 15127
Washington, D.C. 20003-0127   (202-293-8860)

Drunk Driving

o   Mothers Against Drunk Driving (MADD)
669 Airport Freeway
Hurst, TX 76053   817-268-MADD
Victim Line 1-800-438-MADD

o   Remove Intoxicated Drivers (RID)
PO Box 520
Schenectady, NY 12301   (518-372-0034)

o   Students Against Driving Drunk (SADD)
     PO Box 800
     Marlborough, MA 01752 (508-481-3568)

Dying

o   National Hospice Organization
     1901 North Fort Meyer Drive, Suite 402
     Arlington, VA 22209 (703-243-5900)

o   Society for the Right to Die
     250 West 57th St.,
     New York, NY 10107   (212-246-6962)

Funerals

o   Conference of Funeral Service Examining Boards
     520 E Van Trees St.
     PO Box 497
     Washington, IN 47501   (812-254-7887)

o   National Funeral Directors Association
     11121 W. Oklahoma Ave.
     Milwaukee, WI 53227   (414-541-2500)

Head Injury

o   National Head Injury Foundation
     333 Turnpike Road
     Southborough, MA 01772   (508-485-9950)
     (Family Help Line - (1-800-444-NHIF)

o   Sunny Von Bulow Coma & Head Trauma
     Research Foundation
     11 Park Place   Ste. 1601
     New York, NY 10007 (212-732-8767)

Murder

o   Parents of Murdered Children
    100 E. 8th St., Rm. B41
    Cincinnato, OH 45202   (1-800-327-2499, Ext. 4288
    Emergencies (513-721-5683)

o   Concerns Of Police Survivors (COPS)
    16921 Croom Road
    Brandywine, MD 20613   (301-888-2264)
    For families of slain police officers

Sexual Assault

o   National Coalition Against Sexual Assault
    8787 Assault State Street, Suite 202
    East St. Louis, IL 62203   (618-398-7764)

o   Sexual Violence Center
    1222 W. 31st St.
    Minneapolis, MN 55408   (612-824-2864)

Sudden Infant Death Syndrome

o   National SIDS Foundation
    8200 Professional Place, Suite 104
    Landover, MD 20785   (301-459-3388)

o   Counseling & Research Center for SIDS
    PO Box 1997
    Milwaukee, WI 53201 (218-739-5252)

Spinal Cord Injury

o   National Spinal Cord Injury Assn.
    600 W. Cummings Park Ste. 2000
    Woburn, MA 01801 (617-935-2722)
    Help Line 1-800-962-9629

o Spinal Cord Society
   2410 Lakeview Dr.
   Fergus Falls, MN 56537 (218-739-5252)

Suicide

o American Association of Suicidology
   2459 So. Ash
   Denver, CO 80222 (303-692-0985)

o Samaritans
   500 Commonwealth Ave., Kenmore Sq.
   Boston, MASS 02215   24 Hour line (617-247-0220)
                              Teen line (617-247-8050)

Trauma

o American College of Emergency Physicians
   1125 Executive Circle
   Irving, TX 75038   (214-550-0911)

o American Trauma Society
   1400 Mercanfile Lane Ste. 188
   Landover, MD 20785 (1-800-556-7890)

Widowed Persons

o National Association for Widowed People
   PO Box 3564
   Springfield, IL 62708

o THEOS (They Help Each Other Spiritually) Foundation
   1301 Clark Bldg.
   717 Liberty Ave.
   Pittsburgh, PA 15222   (412-471-7779)

FOOTNOTES

Part I

1. Saldana, Theresa. (1986) *Beyond Survival.* New York: Bantam Books, p. 54.

2. **Ibid.**, p. 75

3. Rollin, Betty. (1985) *Last Wish.* New York: Linden/Simon and Schuster. p. 170.

Part II

1. Nicholas Wolterstorff, *Lament for a Son* (Grand Rapids, MI: Wm. B. Eerdsmans Publishing Co., 1987), p.

2. National Committee for Prevention of Child Abuse, Fact Sheet No. 9, *Child Deaths Due to Maltreatment,* April, 1987.

3. American Psychiatric Association, Psychiatric News, *Coalition to Launch Campaign Against Domestic Violence,* by Joan O'Connor, July 3, 1986.

4. *Crimes Against the Elderly,* U. S. Government Printing Office, Washington D.C., 1986.

5. Kate Sheehy, "Battered Women" in the *Atlanta Mirror,* Altoona, PA, July 12, 1986.

6. Janice Harris, "Non-Professionals as Effective Helpers for Weary Social Workers," *The Advocate: Journal of Alpha Delta Mu* 1 (Spring, 1981), pp. 3-17.

Part III

1. Janice Harris Lord, "Survivor Grief Following a Drunk Driving Crash," Death Studies, 11:413-435, 1987.

INDEX

NOTES

ORDER FORM

Pathfinder Publishing
458 Dorothy Ave.
Ventura, CA 93003
Telephone (805)642-9278

Please send me the following books from Pathfinder Publishing:

_____Copies of **Beyond Sympathy** @ $9.95 $_____

_____Copies of **No Time For Goodbyes** @ $8.95 $_____

_____Copies of **Stop Justice Abuse** @ $10.95 each. $_____

                                        Sub-Total $_____

Californians: Please add 6% tax. $_____

Shipping & Handling $_____

                    Grand Total $_____

I understand that I may return the book for a full refund if not satisfied.

Name:_____

Organization:_____

Address:_____

_____ZIP:_____

* **Shipping:** $1.70 for the first book and .35c for each additional book.